*To my mentor, Shabalala, who taught the ancient wisdom of honouring our ancestors.
And to my beloved ancestor, the late Rev. Verrall Johnson, whose larger than life personality demanded a special place in this book.
Because I listened for once, the content has been lifted from the more often mundane to sometimes hilarious - but never dull!!*

© Derek Johnson 2013-11-15
ISBN 978-1-304-62573-1

# Introduction

When I started writing this book, I thought that it would be about the magnificent African Shaman, Shabalala and his influence on my life like a golden cord weaving through almost every event that combined to make me who I am.
And it is true.
But not the whole truth.
   There was also the other side of growing up in the colonial era.
The dark cord, just as valid in intertwining with the light to create a life of a person, both victor and victim of his times.
Perhaps a reflection in microcosm of some of the troubles that continue to plague us all in spite of the changes that have taken place.

   While I was writing parents, friends, acquaintances and yes, even some enemies, popped into my head and insisted that they have their part in the story of Cipolopolo described as faithfully as possible!

I truly thank them for bringing the wonderful memories, so long forgotten, back to life.

# Shabalala

Even though his real name was Shabalala, everyone called him Vegetable because he ran the vegetable gardens on the small farm that I grew up on.
He was also my mentor, who would set the pattern of my life, no matter how I fought the calling.
In the carefree days of brown as berry skin no shirts and bare feet of Northern Rhodesia in the 1950's, a great teacher found a six year old boy and taught him the ancient ways.
It was on a glorious African morning that he first changed my life. I was sitting in a discarded kitchen cupboard carving and thumping the ruined Masonite backing board with a small lipstick holder. Shabalala poked his head into the cupboard and asked in Chilapalapa *Hau, pickanini bwana, eni weana enswa ko lo buletti?*
*Buletti?* No, he was wrong; it was my mother's lipstick not a bullet.
He gently prised the live .22 round from my hand and looked at me in wonderment.
*Wena as eiffa skut wena enswa so!* –You will die if you do this.
He took me by the hand and led me to the shade of a huge avocado tree that towered over our flat roofed house.
*Shala lapa, haekona hamba lapa lo kubodi.* –Stay here; don't go back to the cupboard. Soon the incident was forgotten as a new game formed in my mind and I happily started making roads and miniature houses in the dark damp clay.
Later, after a warm bath heated by the donkey boiler that was made from two forty four gallon drums over a wood fire, I heard my father telling my mother, "Mary, do you know that Vegetable found Derek in those old cupboards

outside playing with these?" He opened his hand revealing a small pile of gleaming bullets.

"Verrall, you must be more careful where you put those things, the kids don't know any better and something could happen to them!"

The next morning I found the cupboards and their contents gone and myself ordered to stay "near Vegetable". Soon I was back in the shade of the avocado tree, surrendered to the wonderful adventures being played out in my mind. Occasionally, Shabalala would appear, stare at me and then fade into his beloved garden. When it was time for him to move to another section, he would coax me away from my special tree with, *"Pickanini bwana, fuga lo manzi pezula lo caroti."* -Little lord, come, water the carrots. Soon the two of us would be busy with watering the garden and looking in wonderment at the way the little plants seemingly sprouted leaves and grew into magnificent orange carrots before our very eyes. On some occasions, when I became bored with the gardens, I would climb onto a 44 gallon drum lying on its side and pretend I was a knight riding a horse. I kicked the sides of the barrel and the two of us charged into the wonderland of heroism and daring-do.

*Hau wena! Bwuya lapa, mena funa wena enswa lo sebenza.* Hey, come here, work with me!

Over the weeks of the school holidays, Shabalala gruffly took me into the wonderland that was the vegetable garden. He would plant, weed and water, coaxing the new life into this world with the love that only a great shaman has for nature. The feel of the earth, the softness of new growth and the smell of the water evaporating off the dark, rich soil surrounded the joy of that marvellous garden. Once on one of my scavenging trips in the nearby trash pit, I found a piece of cloth with stays and hooks attached to it just like a magnificent saddle. I threw it over my metal horse and charged into battle with the black knight. Shabalala chuckled and went back to his work singing a Bemba tune to himself softly and repetitively *Ka luBemba kwali wama and Twamitotela, Twatotela, Twatotela mwe Mfumu – The Bemba country is good and we thank, thank you, thank you Lord.*

I was brought back to the garden with sounds of girlish giggling. There, in our garden were Rosemary and Christina, the two most beautiful girls in the world and the daughters of a neighbouring farmer. My steel horse and I had rescued them many times from the black knight. "You silly boy, what are you doing, sitting on that old girdle!" I didn't know what a girdle was but was certain, by their scorn that it was something embarrassing and it would be a long time before I could even look a girl in the eyes again. Soon the holidays were over and it was back to Mrs. Simms and my standard one classmates. Shabalala, still kept an eye on me, but we did not have time for the garden after the soccer and the travelling to and fro from the farm.

One Sunday, a day when the farm labourers did not work, Shabalala appeared in the back garden glancing around nervously before he spoke; "*Bwuya, mena funa wena bonabulega*". Come, I have something to show you - be quick. We left the back of the house and onto the footpath towards the compound or village for the farm workers. He seemed to relax when the main farmhouse was lost in one of the turns of the path. I wondered what was so special that he had to take me to the village on a Sunday when we both knew that I had been there many times to play with the children of the servants. But we walked by the village without stopping and across the little mound of sand that represented the back border of the farm. We crossed the provincial road and skirted the Rabie homestead, walking in the heavily forested as yet unclaimed part of the lands.

"Where are we going, Shabalala?" He turned and silenced me with his eyes.

The undergrowth was becoming so thick now that we could not walk without pushing aside the plants that reached across to us over the footpath. Soon we crossed the railway line at Kaneki siding, jumped a shallow ditch and I knew we were in the Belgian Congo. Immediately, Shabalala vanished into the bush and I ran to catch up with him. You make noise like elephant! A tree said in broken English. I crept respectfully around the talkative tree to discover Shabalala squatting in front of a sturdy, small bush with broad leaves that looked furry. To my relief I realised that Shabalala had spoken and not the tree when he said. "I speak English you, not chilapalapa, the language of miners. Here we must first talk English, later Bemba."

Although he was staring at the strange plant, he started speaking to me in a tone he had often used before in the vegetable garden when he told the old stories.

"Last night, after singing the beer songs I went to my hut to sleep. The dreams came to me and I saw my Grandfather looking very worried at his fire. I crept on my knees with my head bowed, because he had been a great sangoma before being my grandfather and needed even more respect than most. He said nothing for a very long time and then, "My son, I have a very important task for you. You are to take the white boy and teach him in our ways for he is destined to be a healer in a time when our people will once again rule the land." Shabalala glanced at me both sternly and incredulously, daring me to say something. He shouldn't have worried, I was always entranced at his stories and never wanted to disturb him in case I missed something. "I do not understand this because you are white and an ignoramus!" He sighed, "I will try with this impossible task, but I think we will fail because you know nothing but how to command the servants to do everything that a lazy boy should do for himself!'

Shabalala returned to the strange plant and shook his head regretfully, "This is a powerful herb that was used by my *Icikolwe* –ancestors (Bemba) for many sicknesses, too many people took it and now there is just this one. I cannot use it for medicine now because it grows here and it is forbidden to take from it. I can only protect it."

I was puzzled; "But Shabalala, we can take it just like this." I approached the plant with my hand outstretched.

STOP! The shaman roared and grabbed my hand. He had never touched me before, and should it be discovered, the colonial police would arrest him.

The tears welled up in my eyes and his voice softened as he searched for the English words. "It is the place of the dead and it is forbidden for anyone to take from here."

"Come, we go back". Still sniffling, I followed his quickly vanishing body into the green foliage.

When our homestead was close, he reverted to chilapalapa, *"Wena hakona chela lo bwana ini wena boogile"* – Don't tell you father what you have seen. And then for good measure; *"Wena hakona chela zonke ini wena boogile!"* Don't tell anyone what you have seen.

He left me in the backyard to explain to my mother how my sorry state of clothing and my tear streaked face had come into being.

# A fertile country, lightening and a rigged trial

Everything seemed to grow extraordinarily well in our magnificent country.
Shabalala's green fingers and the vegetable garden notwithstanding, anything that traditionally grew in the tropics would thrive on our farm.
Once, totally entranced in a game, I ran into a Poinsettia tree and a branch coloured like that of an elephant's skin fell to the ground. The broken limb was topped with red leaves and little flowers that looked like day old chicken heads, their new yellow beaks glowing in the late November sunlight.
A milky sap exuded from the lesion. Guiltily, I picked the broken branch up and gently inserted it in the soft soil of a nearby rosebush.

Within a season or two, we had a new, thriving plant.


We had oranges and lemons, peaches and of course mangoes. Litchis, paw paws and bananas flourished. Avocado pears grew like weeds, as Mary used to say.

After running around wildly, one my favourite ways of resting was to lie next to a gooseberry bush and pick the ripe golden berries off one of the plants that my mother always planted next to a brass garden tap. Only the fruit which had an almost translucent outer membrane like a miniature Chinese lantern would be selected. Then, very tenderly, I squeezed this covering and if it was crinkly like dried out parchment, the gooseberry would be plucked. This was certain to give the sweetest taste. Sun warmed juice ran from my lips, down my chin and dripped on my

bare chest, leaving drops of sticky residue against brown skin.
This would later be remedied by a quick dip in one of the forty four gallon drums scattered around our smallholding. Verrall had strategically placed them as water reservoirs for the workers to dip into while irrigating our farm gardens.

Mary had devoted four acres of land to plant a rose garden. Locals scoffed at the ridiculous idea of roses growing in our climate.
Nevertheless, Mary sowed her garden and, with Shabalala's loving attention, she soon had a glorious display of multicoloured flowers preening smugly in the sunlight.

Soon my mother had a thriving business supplying the local florists.

Of course the reason everything grew so well was the heavy rainfall we enjoyed.
With the rain came lightening.
There was a window over the sink in our inside kitchen.
Mom, I think to take a break from the rest of her boisterous and demanding family sometimes would busy herself at the sink with some foamy water and one or two dishes. On this occasion, she was staring out at one of the wondrous storms that seemed to appear from nowhere, rain heavily for a few minutes and then disappear as quickly as it arrived.
Suddenly there was an enormous cracking sound from the kitchen that had us all running to investigate. Mary was standing stock still with her rubber gloved hands held straight up in the air, staring at the floor under a small table opposite the sink.

"Mom, what happened?" She pointed wordlessly in the same direction she was staring.
We looked and there, on the concrete floor, the red rubber basket that mom used to collect vegetables from the garden, lay totally turned inside out.
Again; "Mom, what happened?!!"
"Lightening". She stuttered.
Verrall, now part of the panicky group had decided the best solution would be brandy and was feeding a fully loaded glass to mom's mouth.
"What about the lightening, mom?"
"Mmmmmphf" she replied pushing the brandy glass away.
"I said," glaring at Verrall who was now sipping at the offending glass, "I said lightening came through the window, past my shoulder and turned the basket inside out!"
Impressed we picked the basket up and passed it wondrously from hand to hand.
"Look at the floor!" my sibling cried.
We all stared.
A hole about one and a half inches deep had appeared in the concrete floor.
Verrall finished mom's medicinal brandy with alacrity.


Often, when chickens were required for the pot, Verrall would delegate the selection and slaughter of an unfortunate bird to us.
The three of us would go to the chicken run near mom's outside kitchen and select one of the red feathered birds.

And the chase began.
Catching a chicken is not as easy as one would think... not in our chicken coop anyway. Verrall in his wisdom had decided that it would be more attractive if a false stream

flowed through the cage. It served both a decorative and a functional purpose and he was very proud of his creativity. No amount of protesting allowed him to agree to change. The problem was that the "river" wasn't deep enough to stop any fleeing chicken but just deep enough to splash a few cups full of water on its banks and surrounds every time a fowl forded it.

Chickens are instinctive creatures and as soon as we arrived, they would scatter across Verrall's river to the furthest part of the cage. This wet the earth enough to create a slippery mix that combined with chicken droppings became a thoroughly unpleasant stew of smelly slime. As the chase began and birds sprinkled everywhere throughout the cage, the stew churned even more. Boys and bird, in their haste, were slipping and sliding in the goo until not a square inch of any child was left uncovered in pooh. Our efforts never went unnoticed and soon the two German Shepherds, Janie and Lola, my little cross pug, Gertrude Gesondheid and usually some of the kids from the labourers' village were chorusing their encouragement. The competition between us brothers then became more competitive and our faces set in grim determination to become the first person to capture a chicken.

I would like to say that I sometimes triumphed, but even though I was always optimistic about my chances, I never won the prize of a captured chicken, clutched by the feet and held over my head as I exited the cage in triumph.

I always followed at the back of the conquering procession to our house for the next episode.

This was a tradition we brothers had established.
Once the bird had been captured, one of my elder brothers clasped it under his arm with his hands firmly grasping the poor bird's neck. They would then take their seat in the lounge, leaving a trail of chicken poo and mud into the

pristine room. My position was standing near the dining room door.
We then went into the trial stage of our tradition.
One of the elder siblings became the judge and the other, prosecution. I was always the defence.
No matter how good my high pitched pleas and arguments were, I never won a case. Sentence would then be duly passed and the hapless chicken was led away by the recent prosecutor, now turned executioner, to be beheaded whilst I was left behind to clean up the mess in our lounge.

I was never strong enough to witness the deed and to this day loath the smell and taste of any chicken dish.

# Paraffin on the ceiling

Mom's kitchen was set up for the days before electricity came to the farm.
She had a gas stove, gas toaster and the sink was supplied with hot water fed to a tap above the kitchen sink. This with the complements of a donkey boiler.
A contraption of two forty four gallon drums encased by bricks and a little oven area under the lower drum. When lit, the hot water would rise into the second drum and piped to our house.
Our fridge was a strange device powered by paraffin.
A wonderful concept as paraffin was freely available, even the remotest trading store carried this fuel.
There was, however one drawback. The wick had to be trimmed regularly otherwise the fridge would heat up with alarming haste.
We knew it was time for a trim when black smoke started to billow from the tin flu behind our green painted refrigerator.
It may seem that this was a simple task, but Verrall decided that as paraffin and a flame were involved; only he was permitted to trim the wick.
Eventually a mini ceremony developed. Someone would notice the first wisps of dark smoke emitting from the chimney and my father, on strict instructions, was notified. Inevitably he muttered about "having to do everything myself" and with much sighing he proceeded to the kitchen. His special wick trimming tools were in a drawer that no one was permitted to open. Carefully he would open his drawer and meticulously study each tool, until at

last he decided on the perfect implement - always the same pair of Mary's old sewing scissors.
He then kneeled down at the side of the fridge and peered inside the mysterious innards. Only his bottom would be visible as he bowed lower to examine the recalcitrant wick. The grey flannelled bottom would mutter and there would be a snipping sound. Usually this was followed by a loud "Ouch!" as he burned himself on the glowing wick.
Part two of the ritual then began.
Mom would be summoned. The wounded, moaning Verrall was led to the bathroom and our medicine cabinet with much sympathetic cooing.
Eventually my father reappeared with a huge swab of cotton wool around the offended finger. Said finger being held up prominently for all to see.
Evidence of my father's unselfish sacrifice just for his family to have cool food.
Stage three, the final stage began. Once again each tool in the wick trimming drawer would be studied until a box of lion matches was selected with and audible "Ah!"
Gingerly lowering himself more carefully this time because of his wound, dad once more bent into the bottom pointing position and his voice authoritatively banning the whole family from the kitchen: "in case there is an explosion."
Soon thereafter a satisfied father would reappear with the reassurance that "All was well."
We were then permitted to re-enter the kitchen - until the next wick trimming ceremony was needed.
One day the black smoke appeared just after my parents departed for Ndola. They would not be back for the entire day.
There was only one thing to do- fix it myself.
I marched up to the wick trimming drawer, studied each tool in turn until I selected the scissors. Doing my best to repeat the necessary position so important to a successful

wick trimming. I climbed down on my knees and presented my bottom to Laya, the head houseman. Not sure of the words my father used I just muttered with the same tonal cadence. I stared into the innards. There, in front of me, oily smoke was being discharged from a small fabric wick. Now I did not know the secret process so I would just have to guess.

Next to the wick there was a small round brass wheel. I turned it and fabric appeared from below. Not knowing what was required of the scissors, I decided to remove the entire offending fabric, so I turned the brass wheel until no more fabric came out. I then cut the end and the entire smouldering mess fell onto a tray producing voluminous black smoke that soon engulfed the entire kitchen. Laya, not wanting anything to do with this disaster fled out the kitchen door in the direction of the servants' village.

I, now thoroughly panicked, but very grateful of the lack of other people in the house, fled through the other door in the general direction of my bedroom. I stayed there watching my closed door for evidence of fire damage. Finally, I decided that it was safe to leave my refuge. I gingerly walked back and inspected the fridge. Fortunately the fire had gone, but the proof of the recent disaster covered everything in the kitchen from ceiling to floor. Laya was there, scrubbing the soot away. He glared at me and banned me from playing with anything to do with fire again - ever.

Fortunately he managed to clean everything barring a small patch above the fridge by the time my parents returned home.

Mary blamed Verrall for the mess as only he ever trimmed the fridge wick and I admitted to nothing.

It was not long afterwards that a diesel driven generator appeared. At last we had power together with a shiny new white electric refrigerator.

# The Shaman.

I had learned to sit very quietly outside the sacred circle until summoned.
A cry of the black cheeked lovebird danced with the calling of the forest doves and finally mingled with all the bush sounds. The great Bemba shaman, my teacher, whom I knew as Shabalala and who I had known all the seven years of my short life, sat absolutely still in the small opening in the Congolese forest. He was squatting on his haunches with the smell of the sacred smoke still lingering in the air.
 "Come, Cipolopolo, join me" He had given me the Bemba name for bullet after finding me playing with live .22 rounds over a year ago.
I respectfully approached from behind, as I had been taught, on my knees and with my head bent. When I was just behind him and I faced the big *mbango* tree.
"Today we are going to learn the way to protect ourselves from the evil ones who caste bad spells." He took two of the calabash from the array of containers
stacked neatly on his left and pored black sand from the one onto the kaross lying on the grass. He then poured an equal amount of dark brown sand from the other. With his bone-wand he mixed the two thoroughly, all the while spitting into the concoction. He then took two dried leaves from the *mbango* tree and ground them into the mix with a round stone. "The *mbango* tree wood is almost the hardest of all the trees in the forest and we place its leaves into our medicine for strength".
The whole mix was poured into a deep bowl containing water and cow's urine and once again mixed thoroughly.
'This is the poison of the evil ones", He pointed at his concoction. We must take a small part of this and rub it on

our skin until no parts of our bodies are seen by the evildoers." It was believed by Bemba Witchdoctors that only equal and stronger potions were powerful enough to fight spells cast by witches.

The N'Ganga (*Bemba, Witchdoctor or Doctor who cures witches curses*)then took a roll of tobacco from his pocket, chose a few leaves and placed them in a fork of a small branch pointing away from the tree's massive trunk. "The spirits love to smoke tobacco and this is our thanks to the holy one who lives here."

My mentor had a great reverence for all living things, be-it humans, animals or vegetation. He made a special effort to acknowledge the spirits residing in

the surrounding trees and animals. Before starting any ceremony, in addition to offering tobacco, the N'Ganga would call on the *Ngulu (nature spirits)* watching to bless our efforts but always with the admonition-"Leza is our god and must always be honoured, for without him there is no magic."

"Remember, Cipolopolo, never forget to honour the gifts of our ancestors or to fight angry spirits unless you are protected and your own spirit is strong."

His eyes glazed and he started chanting.

I knew that the lesson was finished and it was time to go.

I backed away until my whole body had left the sacred area. Just as well because the clouds were heavy and it would surely rain soon.

The joy of being free and away from the sharp eyes of my teacher soon had me running through the dense forest, the leaves tapping against my khaki shirt and shorts in applause of the exuberance of a free young boy. My bare feet pattered a slip slap tattoo on the clay foot path until I came to a large opening in the forest just as the rain started to pour down.

A joyous yelp burst from my lips as I raced towards the torrent of water which did not move but seemed to dare me to leap into its cool wet embrace. I stopped just before the wall of water. It made me feel just like Shabalala to be able to stand and face the rain without getting wet. Slowly I raised my right arm into the downpour and watched in wonder as rivulets streamed past my elbow and onto the ground. I gingerly stuck my dirty face into the water and giggled as the drops tickled my nose. My resistance to the rain cracked and I dived into the cooling stream. Within a second I was drenched and was certain that when I got home my grandmother, a large Dutch lady, who we all called Cuckoo was waiting to punish a very wet young boy. It didn't matter, though; the cooling water was worth it. As quickly as it had arrived, the downpour finished and I trotted through a mysterious and hazy mist of steam that arose from the still hot earth. All the undergrowth glistened with joy to be rid of dust coats accumulated since the last rainfall. Wonderful fresh smells unique to the Northern Rhodesian forest energised my sense of smell while insects and small animals of the forest called their exuberant thanks to a generous god. My khaki clothes soon warmed up and were nearly dry long before I even saw our homestead.

Yellow grass on newly built wattle and daub huts greeted me as I crossed the back border of our farm and walked through the rapidly growing village. Recently employed labourers had begun to join the established workforce as Verrall's dairy herd grew.

Soon, new friendships would be made as families settled and I surreptitiously joined lunch time feasts of sudsa and kapenta.

"Cipolopolo!" an older child called, his familiarity with the *pickanini bwana* shocking the new arrivals.

I smiled and greeted Laya's son in my version of chilapalapa, "Eh, *sambonani, Gora! Mina as bwuya futi ko puza lo kapenta ka wena!*" (I see you, Gora, I will return to eat kapenta with you).
The last hundred yards to the farm was through sparkly elephant grass and then past Shabalala's dynamic vegetable garden, seemingly growing in front of my eyes as I trotted by.

By the time Cuckoo spotted me, there were no more wet patches on my clothes.

I was safe from her fury.

## Michael, the Bishop and mangoes

My best friend, Michael, lived on the farm next door. We had a unique way of calling each other. Rather than use the farm party line telephone, we chose the largest and closest ant heap, clambered to the summit and yelled at the top of our voices until a satisfactory response came from next door.
The only problem was that Janie and Lola, the two German shepherds thought that this was the perfect opportunity to join their pack in calling. The busy morning sounds of the local fauna shattered every time we had a need to contact each other….. "MICHAAAAAL…!!!" I would yell.
"ARRROOOO….!!" The two dogs responded.
"MICHAAAAAAEL, AROOOO, MICHAAAAAEL, AROOOO!" Sometimes he was not in earshot, so I would bellow; "MIIIIIICHAAAAEl!!!" The dogs on hearing my increase in volume, responded, "AROOOOOO, BWOOF, BWOOF!"
 One morning Verrall was entertaining the Lord Bishop of Hereford in his study. His grace was a houseguest for a few days. He had come to the farm for some quiet time away from a busy schedule as an honoured guest to the diocese of Rhodesia and Nyasaland.
I don't know what was being discussed, but I do remember a red faced father furiously striding up the path towards my ant heap.
"DEEEREKKK!!!" he shouted. Janie and Lola, sensing that something exciting was happening, charged up the path behind an incensed Verrall, "AROOOOO, BWOOOF, AROOOOO" they chorused.
"DEEEREKK'" responded Michael, at last in earshot.
"MICHAAAEL" roared Verrall now almost apoplectic, "JANIELOLA" brushing at the excited dogs now dancing at

his heals. Well aware of the impending consequences to Verrall's anger, I scurried down the ant heap and joined Michael on the forest lined path between our two farms.
"DEREKMICHAEL!!!" My furious father exploded.
"AROOOOOBWOOFAROOOOBWOOF" the thoroughly excited dogs called.
"VERRALLLLLL!" a feminine voice cried as my mother appeared up the path. "Don't you know that the Bishop is trying to rest?
"But Derek….." protested my father.
Just then the honourable and esteemed member of the British House of Lords appeared, red faced from his effort to join the commotion by the ant heap.
Janie and Lola, now beyond any sense, leaped on the cassocked cleric, their muddy feet leaving streaked trails up and down the purple garment. Verrall dived at the dogs, catching their collars whilst attempting to stand at attention and apologise at the same time' "the boy…." He sputtered not quite finishing his sentence.
The bishop stood up, his hand gently on Mary's shoulder, "I think that's enough excitement for me. Come, Verrall, lets try to be less boisterous on our journey back to your delightful study".
   My lord the bishop of Hereford guided my two now slightly frustrated but no longer angry parents back towards the farmhouse.
Surreptitiously, he glanced at the two wide eyed little boys peeping from behind an mbango tree and winked.

   That evening, as I tiptoed past the study, a plummy English voice called from the depths of my father's favourite chair, "Derek, would you like to join me?"
   Intimidated, I obeyed.

22

The bishop was dressed in a pair of shorts and a brightly coloured short sleeved shirt. He smiled kindly, "Please, sit down here, next to me, I need your advice."
My chest expanded to bursting point as I sat next to the great man.

He picked a book up that was laying on the side table next to him; it was importantly titled 'A manual of Greek mythology." He opened it to a bookmarked page. "It says here, "So Jason, joined by the Argonauts, began his great adventure in search of the Golden Fleece. What do you think of Jason - was he hero or anti hero?"
Even at my tender age of seven Verrall had made sure that the swashbuckling adventuring heroes of Greek mythology had come to life. I had sat in this study and listened with bated breath as my father read aloud from that very same book. I knew the story of the fickle and incompetent Jason, and thankfully was able to answer the bishop with some level of proficiency. Outwardly showing no surprise he began the first of many debates where, in the guise of "advice" the bishop instilled the love of the classics which to this day I treasure amongst my fondest memories. Sometimes, we would debate the ways of the world and always in a kindly manner, he taught a small boy of the importance of the love of education, but more importantly the love and respect of our fellow man, no matter who or how old he was.

When the bishop left our farm for the last time, He said, as if he were addressing an old friend, "If you are ever in Hereford, please come visit me at the palace". An invitation, to my immense regret, I never took up.

It was mango season and the two hundred trees lining the driveway to the farm were dropping their ripe juicy fruits onto the hot soil. The smell of the kidney mangos especially scented the air as Michael and I walked down the quarter mile it took to reach the Ndola / Mufulira road. Our bare feet luxuriated in the cool sand filling the tracks on either side of the *middelmannetjie*. (The ridge between the tracks made by car wheels).

About two thirds of the way down the road there, in front of us, was the strangest of sights. A big bright blue van with a large wooden crate instead of a back was parked under a tree while two men were busily loading mangos into its open back.

Hey! Michael and I chorused with our high pitched seven year old voices, *"Ini wena enswa!"*- What are you doing! *"Eh, bwanas, mena funa lo mango kolo pusa kupela."* -Eh, I want some mangoes to eat, that's all, squeaked the raggedly clad individual, his surprised voice replied emerging from under a shapeless and very the half full crate." *Mena tutile pickanini kupela! Mena as niga wena mali skut wena haekona chela lo baba ko wena!"* - I only took a few. I will pay for them if you don't tell your father. Sensing a business opportunity to enrich the family fortune, I demanded he pay sixpence, but because, I was asking for so much money, I offered him the chance to fill the wooden back of his van at no extra charge. Felt hat and his even shabbier partner wasted no time in loading the rest of the mangoes. He hastily offered sixpence to me and the two of them, the blue truck and mangoes vanished in a cloud of oily smoke.

We climbed into one of the trees with a mango apiece and lolled on separate branches pridefully deciding that when we grew up we would build a business empire together. Later that day, after boring with our world-wide business enterprise, leading cavalry charges and piloting fighter planes, it was time to go home, Michael to the farm next door and I to present the grimy sixpence proudly to Cuckoo.

"We are lucky that boy didn't think to sell the cattle as well!" Cuckoo's voice seeped through my bedroom door where I had been banned until my father returned. "You must teach him to understand to never sell my chutney and jam ingredients again! And for NOTHING!! Yes," She decided,
"He needs at least six smacks with this sjambok - give it to him now, or I will". She slapped the vicious rawhide whip onto her left hand menacingly.
"DEREK! Get out here, my father called." I gingerly opened the bedroom door and came out onto the front veranda, my head hung as pathetically as possible, "I, I, just......" and then I saw my father's face. He was standing with his back to his mother attempting to look stern, but not hiding his mirth very well. "Next time I catch you doing something so silly again, I will ask Cuckoo to use her sjambok on your bottom!" he admonished.

All was forgiven.

# Cuckoo, corporal punishment and unlearned lessons

Cuckoo, Verrall's mother, and my grandparent, was a formidable old lady. Of Dutch descent, she would occasionally visit her relatives in Amsterdam, Holland for a few months at a time. For safekeeping, She left her ford Popular parked in the garage of our small farm.

This was too good a chance to miss.
We had watched Cuckoo carefully when she delivered her precious vehicle to my father's safekeeping. She handed the keys to Verrall and he took them to his study and hid them behind the cowboy books that lined one wall. At Sundowner time, when all the adults had gathered around the tennis court, I sneaked into my father's study and nicked Cuckoo's keys.

The next day, just as the adults disappeared down the road on their way to Ndola to work, Michael and I raced to the garage, our hearts pumping with excitement at the thought of driving a car for the first time.

The problem was that neither of us had sufficient training or stature to drive a car.

Starting was easy and because Cuckoo had parked her popular facing outwards. Moving forward was merely a matter of releasing the handbrake and pushing the accelerator down. Our major issue of course was the fact that we were too short to control the car individually. We decided that Michael would steer and I would push the pedals from my seated position in the foot well.

It all went reasonably well with Michael shouting "faster, faster or slower, slower." I wasn't sure, however, which

26

pedal was the brake and which was the clutch, so I thought it best to leave both alone. With the engine screaming for mercy, we made our way down the drive.
Michael, realising that we were picking up too much speed, yelled: "brakes!"
I lifted my hand off the accelerator, convinced that would get us into a controllable speed- it did not. By this time we were on the downhill part of the road, picking up speed all the time as the mango trees whizzed by. In his desperation, he decided that the only way to stop would be to turn off the road and gently roll into a mango tree.

Unfortunately, there was no gently about it and the now speeding car slammed into a tree with an hysterical engine roaring until it decided that it had had enough and thankfully stalled. Green mangos, leaves and small twigs were still raining on the black car's roof as Michael yanked the door open; his eyes wide with shock and terror, his brown bare feet rapidly pumping as he hit the ground.

He did not stop running and the last glimpse I had of him was his Khaki shorts disappearing into the bush in the general direction of the Grey farm.

Although I tried manfully, I couldn't satisfactorily explain how Cuckoo's car was buried into the now depleted umbrella of a mango tree. I would like to say Verrall found this prank amusing, but soon discovered the extent of his displeasure when he sentenced me to six of the best on my bottom.

That same bottom received another six, compliments of Cuckoo's sjambok when she returned from Holland, to discover the dents in the front mudguard had been caused by a small and now terrified but unrepentant grandson.

In the 1950's when corporal punishment was regarded as the correct method to reprimand recalcitrant children, my father had a never varying routine. First he would say; "go

get a stick!" And then when we returned with the instrument of torture, he would have us bend over his bed and proceed to give us six of the best.
Never more, never less.
My brother and I developed the science of stickology. We would spend many hours debating the merits of different shapes, sizes and length of the various sticks lying around the back yard and their relative effect on our backsides. The vexing question as to whether a flexible stick would be less painful than the unbending variety. No matter what we chose though, it was always a very painful experience.
During one of our technical discussions it was decided that if the stick were to break at just the right moment of contact with our bottoms, the pain would be minimal.

In the woodpile, next to the donkey boiler, there was a large pile of cut bamboo sticks. We decided that the best way to apply our science was to cut through all the knots until there was very little wood holding the sticks together. It took many hours with borrowed hacksaw blades appropriated from my father's workshop to saw through each and every knot. We then rubbed mud and sawdust into the cut lines to disguise our handiwork.
Inevitably the day of punishment arrived. "Go get a stick!' bellowed my father. Shortly after, I arrived with the adjusted instrument of torture. "Bend over!' He brought the cane down with a well aimed and carefully calculated force. To my father's surprise, the bamboo rod shattered. "Go get another stick!' he demanded.

When the next stick shattered and my shoulders were shaking with mirth an almost apoplectic father, probably to spare my life, kicked me out.

Later when he was able to, he asked, "Derek, why do you boys try me so?"

I replied, "Dad, if I did something wrong, why beat me, why not tell me what I have done and I won't do it again?"
"You know," he replied thoughtfully, "You are right."
And he never raised his hand to me again – much to my brothers' disgust as they continued to be punished in the same old way!

Shabalala never needed to even threaten punishment; his furious eyes were enough to devastate me back to good behaviour.
I had been practising the rituals that he had taught on our many trips into the Congo and decided to mix the protection muti. Soon, though I was not entirely convinced that the mixture was correct, I had a foul smelling mixture bubbling in one of my mother's consul bottling jars. "What you going to use that for?' his well known voice asked from behind me.
I was no longer surprised at his uncanny ability to appear without any warning. "I am just trying to make what you taught me'. His eyes were enough to have me carefully dig a hole in the soil away from my beloved avo tree and bury the potion. "You never make muti unless for making better", he chided.

On a particularly hot day we had been mixing potions and preparing rituals for Shabalala's clients for a few hours and the first few rumblings of hunger and thirst were becoming louder and louder . I didn't worry because the rituals and new knowledge excited and fascinated me. There was no time to stop until my stomach made a particularly loud rumble.
"Cipolopolo, it is time to rest and eat." I shook my head; "I am fine let's just finish this task."
Shabalala beckoned, "Come, I wish to tell you of Headman Kasaru."

The promise of a good story had me up and seated in front of my teacher post haste.

"Not so long ago, there was a well respected man who was a headman from Tumbuka called Mr. Kasaru. He was summoned by the white man district commissioner. Now the village was about 15miles walk away from the commissioner's office and headman Kasaru would have to set out early in the morning. Impatient to leave he ignored his wife's pleas to wait until he had a good *nshima* meal. (A meal cooked from plain mealie-meal) and set off briskly in the hot sun. When he arrived, tired and thirsty, there were long lines of people waiting to see the commissioner and he would have to wait his turn. Before long his eyes glazed and he collapsed.

He was fortunate because Mr. Kasaru had a daughter-in-law who lived not too far away. She splashed water on his face and fed him *nshima* which soon revived the hapless headman.

The people said, *"Njara nkhamtengo, yikatonda a Kasaru."* Which means; "hunger is as tough as a tree, Headman Kasaru succumbed to it."

Now, Cipolopolo, eat!"

A lesson I should have learned, but sadly did not pay enough attention to, and, in later life, as a sufferer of hypoglycaemia, I have been forced to acknowledge the wisdom of my teacher's words!

# Essential transport

My two older brothers possessed twenty eight inch BSA bicycles. These shiny black machines, ubiquitous to Africa, gave my siblings a mobility I could only envy.
"Dad," I whined, "even Michael has a bicycle."
Verrall grunted, "We'll see."
This usually meant; "Never!" But I knew better than to persist.
I stormed out of the house in search of my mentor. Perhaps he would have a sympathetic ear.

Shabalala was singing softly to himself as he toiled in his much-loved vegetable garden. For maximum effect I stomped my feet, kicking up dust whilst sighing melodramatically. I flounced to the forty four gallon drum closest to the shaman and sat down with a thud.

Shabalala ignored me.

I remained on the drum and banged my heals against its metal sides. I shook my head and said Eh! Eh! Eh! As I had seen the villagers do so often when they were upset.

Shabalala ignored me.

Seeing that I was not getting attention, I finally gave up and joined him in tending the vegetables.
I worked silently next to him, his gentle singing soothing the hurt away. The rich soil which so often gave us such spectacular vegetables massaged my hands as I dug in the beds with my fingers. Aromatic aromas of the slightly damp earth mixed with a clean chlorophyll tang of carrots, beets and peas.

"You are asking the wrong way." My mentor finally said, adjusting the *mthambo* bark-string of a recalcitrant pea vine.
"Have I not taught you that you will always receive what you need?"
"Yes, Shabalala, but..."
"You do not question, your needs are always known. For your wants, you only have to ask the ancestors."
"Your wants will be rewarded if you please them."
He turned to attend to the *mthambo* of yet another misbehaving pea vine.
The matter was closed.
The next morning, I sat under my Avo tree and silently asked the ancestors to please make Verrall's heart soften. I knew that I didn't need a bicycle but I *really wanted* one.

Nothing happened.

"Shabalala, the ancestors did not give me my bicycle!" I complained.
He thought on this for a while, "Did you ask properly?"
He handed me a small pinch of tobacco and smiled.
Thanking him, I rushed back to the avo tree. I asked again, this time remembering my manners and first honoured the guardian spirit of that space by carefully placing the tobacco in a fork of two large branches.

Nothing happened.

Until the morning of my birthday.
As I opened my eyes, there, next to a red painted twenty six inch bicycle, stood my parents.
"Happy birthday!" they chorused.

## Mary, the outside kitchen and Happy the bull.

Catherine Burnett known to us as "Aunty Cats" would share the cooking with my mother in the outside kitchen nearly every weekend. Most Saturday mornings, her ancient yellow Ford appeared coughing and wheezing up the driveway, the chrome headlights winking in the sunlight from their mounts above the front mudguards.

The outside kitchen was in a long, low bag washed building built with Kimberly bricks. Its white painted walls were offset by an aging grey asbestos roof.

There were three rooms, all facing the back of our farmhouse. The generator room, with its open gaps in the walls was on one end, next to a long granadilla vine. Alongside this room, my father had his workshop crammed with tools, pieces of wood, steel and uncountable delights. Knowing boys, Verrall had padlocked this room with a large chain bolted firmly to a wooden doorframe so that we could only peer longingly through the dusty window without causing any damage. Of course, it wasn't too long before we had discovered the hidden key!
 Next to the workshop mom had her outside kitchen.
 This was the engine room where Aunty Cats and Mary baked homemade biscuits, jams and breads. They canned fruit, marmalade and pickles in glass consul bottles of various sizes.
Christmas cakes and pudding also appeared magically from this room.
 Mom would collect tickeys (three pence coins) throughout the year and in November, place them, together with one sixpence coin into an aluminium pot and boiled them for an

hour on her large wood burning stove. Aunty Cats wrapped each now sterilized coin in silver paper and mom inserted them into the pudding mix. Christmas day saw us eating as many helpings of pudding as we could stuff into our already bloated stomachs in a desperate competition to find the sixpence and as many tickeys as possible.
 On the outside of the kitchen, there were pens that occasionally held pigs, chickens or even sheep. Inside, wooden shelves held metal bins with flour, sugar and many other mysterious ingredients. Mom's wood-fired stove stood in pride of place next to the stainless steel
table. It had two green enamelled oven doors with four iron plates on top. If one needed to adjust the burning wood beneath the plates, an iron, chistle like tool, hung on a piece of string next to the stove for just such an eventuality.

The various pots pans, baking trays and kitchen tools were shelved on racks below the table and on a wall. A well used apron with faded roses and a frill that had seen better days hung on a nail hammered into the big wooden "Z" on the door.
 I spent many Saturday mornings sitting on the worn stone kitchen step, waiting for anything lickable while delicious cooking smells wafted through the door.  Sometimes I was lucky enough to be presented with leftovers in the decorated beige mixing bowl. I would scoop the delicious sweet mixtures up with damp fingers and then lick the saccharine goo with much smacking and slurping into my mouth.
 I never returned the bowl until its white glazed inside was sparkling clean!
 One day mom and Cats told me they were going for a walk and disappeared around the back of the building.

Curious to see if I was missing anything, I followed and immediately my nose was assailed by the sweet smell of cigarette smoke.
There they were, furtively swapping a cigarette from mouth to mouth. Pointlessly, they flapped at the smoke on each exhale. Mom turned to see me standing by a derelict chicken pen. Emotions of surprise, horror and guilt crossed Mary's face. To catch an adult misbehaving was indeed a rare thing, a moment to be savoured.
But not for long....
"Don't you dare tell your father!" yelped my mother guiltily. I never had a problem with smoking because Shabalala had taught me how the ancestors loved tobacco. It was, however, the first time that I saw her as human and not just a mom – her secret was safe with me.
Verrall, a vehement and vociferous non smoker, believed his wife was free of the filthy habit until his dying day!

Happy was the most aggressive and feared of all the animals on our farm. A thoroughbred Jersey bull, he was kept in his own stable and tethered by a long chain to a ring in his nose. He would be put among the cows only to mate and then returned to his stable, always with respect and always with a bull-hook to his nose ring.

On one occasion, he managed to bend the pole in the centre of the stable enough to allow him to reach the stable wall. By the time the workers managed to restrain him away from the wall, Happy had punched a huge hole through the wattle and daub with his horns and forehead.

We never found out what happened, but somehow Happy had managed to rip his nose-ring off and had escaped from the stable yard. A commotion in the driveway attracted us and we were confronted by the strangest sight. Happy was standing under a mango tree glaring at the labourers who were attempting to force him back to his pen by throwing

mangoes at the maddened bull. He charged his tormentors and they ran yelling to the nearest of the mango trees. The terrified men scrambled up the small trees screaming for help. They appeared as huge black ravens perched precariously amongst the thin branches. To my brothers and I this was the funniest sight and we squealed with mirth.
My father appeared to investigate what all the noise was about. Taking the situation in, he decided that, like the labourers, the only solution to control Happy was to fling the green kidney mangoes at a now frustrated and enraged Happy.
The bull turned and eyed my father. Verrall proved to be able to move as fast as the labourers. Even though we had never seen him run like that before, my father was definitely unable to outrun a maddened bull with his nose ripped and blood streaming down his jaw. Just before my terrified parent reached the safety of a small hut next to a large ant-heap, Happy caught him from behind and almost nonchalantly flicked his head. My father landed in the hut in a most spectacular way, but our joyous laughter was quickly silenced by a furious paternal glance.
Happy, now seemingly satisfied with his handiwork, haughtily allowed the still shaking staff to guide him back to his stable. The sight of him trotting stiff legged, with his head held high and followed by a bevy of cowed farm labourers, the dust from their feet gently rising among the banana trees remains with me to this day. I must admit, though, I am not sure who the labourers were more terrified of, Verrall or Happy!

Verrall was very proud of the fact that his herd of Jersey cows was the most Northern of the S.A. Jersey registered brand. These cows had been ordered on one of our trips to South Africa and with much fanfare arrived in Ndola a few weeks later. The small commercial dairy supplied many of the townsfolk and some of the local farmers. My father decided that it was time for us to learn to be "proper farm boys" and we were led to the milking parlour to learn the trade of milking a cow. Jenny, the matriarch of our herd was duly brought into the stall and had the ankle chains attached to her feet.

I prayed for my brother to be first selected as Jenny and I had had a run in when she butted my back and knocked me onto the cow-pat splattered ground.

"Derek, come try" Boomed my father.

Tentatively I placed my small bottom on the awaiting stool and touched one of Jenny's teats with the tip of my finger.

"No boy, this is how it is done". Verrall reached in from behind the chained legs, grasped two of the teats and began tugging manfully.

Dutifully two streams of milk appeared on each downward pull and with a tinny sound like hard rain hitting a corrugated iron roof, began to fill the milk bucket.

Jenny, sensing the authoritative hand of a pro, immediately lifted her tail and dumped a curly ice cream shaped pat on my father's bald head.

Bewigged in cow poo, my irate father attempted to add dignity to the occasion, "And that boy's is the lesson – never stand behind a cow if you want to milk her". With that, he stood up and marched off towards the house, his brown wig starting its inevitable journey down his neck towards the ground.

We did not dare to screech with laughter until his dignified figure had completely disappeared.

# Dairy antics

I loved spending time in the dairy. The wood slatted building held many fascinations. Stainless steel was everywhere in the spotless room. Tables standing on the highly polished concrete floor gleamed brightly. A smell of fresh milk and Jeyes Fluid permeated everything. But the duel spouted separating machine held a particular charm for me. When fresh milk was poured into the large funnel atop this device, and the handle was turned, milk appeared magically from a lower valve whilst fresh cream dispensed from the upper spout. Both were decanted into glass bottles and then sealed with a wax disc that fitted perfectly into the top of the bottle's neck. The cows produced so much milk that there always was excess. Verrall used this to make cottage cheese. As a result little muslin bags of maturing cottage cheese were always hanging from wire runners on the back veranda next to our kitchen.
But more importantly, because of his cheese production, I thought he never really kept control of the volume of milk.

Just as well because I had a secret.

Aunty Betsy, returning from one of her trips to Switzerland, had brought a small gift for me. It was a cow's horn with a small whistle attached to the narrow end. When this device was blown, a sound resembling the noise cattle made when they were dropping a calf was emitted.
When Verrall and Mary were away in Ndola, I blew this fiendish instrument and the village children would come running egged on by Janie and Lola's barking. We all met at the dairy where half pint bottles of milk were dispensed. We sat under the granadilla creeper and drank our bounty, white rings of milk appearing around our mouths.

38

The vegetable garden was next to our black painted dairy and Shabalala would keep watch in case Cuckoo or my brothers investigated.
One day, however, my teacher had briefly walked away and Cuckoo suddenly appeared.
"What are you doing!!" she yelled.
In horror we hid the bottles behind our backs and tried to look as innocent as possible.
"Nothing." We chorused.
"You've been stealing milk!" My grandmother cried triumphantly, "I can see the milk around your mouths!"
As one we wiped our mouths with dirty sleeves.
"No, Cuckoo, we have done nothing." I brazened.
"You've just wiped it away!" she spluttered, "Wait until your father gets home!" And she stormed off accompanied by little boys titters from behind grubby hands.

Verrall arrived home later that day and Cuckoo's indignant voice could be heard; " .....and they just wiped it away!"
"Don't worry, mom, I'll deal with it."
And he did.

I was given permission to ration one half pint of milk per day per village child.

# Critters and a small miracle

My brothers each owned a Daisy BB gun. Their pellet guns looked just like the Remington rifles I had seen in cowboy movies.
One day, Michael and I managed to appropriate these magnificent weapons.
We became the great hunters as we set off into the trees between our two farms. Fearlessly we stalked huge game, shooting herds of elephants, buffalo and even lion. Soon, though, we tired of these games and decided we needed a real target. We loaded our rifles
with the little lead mushroom shaped pellets. Their hollowed out centres perfectly shaped to allow a blast of air pressure to propel the missiles through a paper target at fifty meters. As silently as possible we crept through the bush, our eyes and ears on full alert.
Without success.
The birds colourfully flitted from tree to tree, their calls warning any creature before we had a chance to even see them.
As the morning aged and the sun's heat began to take its energy toll, we became desperate. No matter how hard we tried the birds strident alarms saved whoever happened to be in our way.
 We decided that we could not return without a trophy, so any creature would do.

Of course, the birds.

Michael and I crouched down into the grass and waited for our torturers to settle. The lust of the hunt was upon us and Shabalala's lessons about the value of all life became an almost silent whisper in my heart.

Just enough for me to have a mild niggling in my gut.

Yes, there was a bird. The excitement rose like a hot larva flow up from my belly and into my brain. I was no longer an apprentice healer; I was only focussed on the kill.
Carefully, as if we were dancing a prerehearsed duet, we raised our pellet guns together, sighted the bird and fired in unison.
The little creature appeared to fly away at first. But no, it was the impact that had dislodged him off his branch. With wings folded the kill somersaulted down until it landed almost gently on a tuft of long green grass.
Michael and I rushed to where the little body was lying, our eyes like saucers. We weren't able to look at each other as a small rivulet of blood stained the beautiful yellow and blue feathers. I tossed the pellet gun down as if it had suddenly grown thorns. Michael followed suit.
The tears began to flow as I realised what I had done and I know my friend felt the same way because he took his pocket knife out and silently dug a small grave. It wasn't necessary to say anything because our hearts began a mourning process that engraved a lifelong loathing of the hunt into our very souls.
That small burial mound in a remote corner of northern Zambia continues to remind me to this day of that dark part in my soul that will never be released again.

In Northern Rhodesia, the army ants were amongst the most feared of creatures. Although their pitch black bodies were only about one and a half inches long, occasionally, in uncountable numbers they would merge into a long column sometimes one hundred and twenty feet long by three and a half feet wide.

They always marched in a straight line, consuming everything in their path. There was no way to stop or deter them. All one could do was to get out of their path.
For some reason they were rumoured to not like crossing rubber or oil, so when the black silent and menacing column appeared, the whole family retreated to the car in the hope that the ants' dislike of rubber was enough to protect us. Another solution, however, had to be found for our caged rabbits. The four legs of the hutch were mounted in tin cans filled with old motor car oil.

   Inevitably, one fateful day the army ants arrived and marched straight up the slasto stoned path, under the white columns of the pergola and onto our farmhouse's front door.
The house servants shouted warnings and my mother; Mary, scooped us up and, together with blankets and torches we fled to the car.
 Verrall meanwhile kept a rearguard defensive retreat behind us with his blowtorch temporarily slowing the rampaging army. With flames ripping from the brass barrel of the blowtorch into the leading soldier ants, the small ant bodies exploded in the heat. This heroic measure managed to give us enough time to clamber into the family vehicle, with a very angry father slapping at the few insects that were able to get past the torch and start nipping at his legs with their tiny mouths.
 The next day we followed the destructive trail into our home. All exposed food that had been in the army's path had been eaten. The ants had emerged from the farmhouse through the back door and into the farmyard.
   With a sinking feeling in my stomach I stared at the silent Hutch where my rabbits, Footfoot and Thumpy lived. Without crying out I ran to the cage and saw that the ravenous army had formed a tiny bridge with ant bodies

across the oil. I peered through the chickenwire, my eyes beginning to well with tears.
Because all that remained of my pets were two clean skeletons on the hutch floor.

As in most colonial homes at the time, amongst the usual menagerie of cats, dogs and rabbits, we had a caged budgie. Although he was a general pet, I was always attracted by his happy call and bright eyes.
One day, he had somehow managed to escape from his small wirey prison and had flown away. With the demise of Footfoot and Thumpy still fresh in my mind I fled to my favourite refuge, the avo tree.
Tearily, I decided to try to speak to spirit as I had been taught.
"Great father Leza, I make this offering to you and your humble servant begs for the safety of my bird, please keep him safe with all your other charges." I laid my favourite rubber soldier on a bed of tobacco and set fire to the parcel, hoping that the spirits would accept this very precious gift.

There are many possible logical reasons, but to a small, sad boy, when the budgie landed on my shoulder, sat there for a few moments and then flew away; I experienced my first encounter with magic.

I also developed a lifelong loathing of the caging of creatures that should always be free.


Verrall decided to build a fishpond on one side of our farmhouse. It had two adjoining figure of eight ponds each eight foot in diameter. At the head of the first pool of water, he built a small waterfall and planted succulents in fertile black soil strategically located amongst the cemented rocks.

Water gurgled down three feet and splashed into the first figure of eight. Bubbles burst amongst large water lily leaves and the slight current caused gleaming goldfish tails to ripple gently.

At night, this Idyll transformed into Verrall's nemeses. Every sunset a myriad of frogs, large and small, began their mating calls.

Wanting to listen to the gently bubbling waterfall, Verrall had built his pond just a few yards away from my parents' bedroom. Without fail, our late night's sleep was regularly interrupted by various ingenious traps crashing and snapping, usually followed by a gleeful, "Got the buggers this time!"

The silence most often lasted for about twenty minutes and then....

"Croaaaaak!" And the symphony would continue in full voice as if nothing had happened.

Our delicious anticipation was always rewarded with choice language followed by the promise of a better trap the next night.

One afternoon my parent arrived back home from work in Ndola, a giant contraption wielded together from salvaged car parts emerged from the Vauxhall's boot. Dangling from its underside was a weird cage- like apparition made from bird wire.

Triumphantly, Verrall announced that the "frog problem" was solved. We were to take this contraption and scoop all the green menaces from the pond. After much hunting and excited yelps we had the frogs caught in the now disassembling contraption. Carefully carrying the still caged and unwanted creatures to the car, we proceeded to the Hunkin's farm about two miles away and without ceremony dumped the hapless creatures into their dam.

44

Uncle Bob Hunkin was convinced the devil had something to do with his sleepless nights as so many frogs appeared in his dam all at the same time.

Even though I had never heard the word, the gods used me as their instrument of karma.
Unbeknown to Verrall, my collection of frogs' eggs had just hatched in the consul jar borrowed from my mother's pantry. It was alive with tadpoles and they needed a new home...

# The leopard, the loo and a lion

As in most homes of that time we had no indoor facilities. Our loo, made of corrugated sheeting was located behind an ant heap about twenty yards from the back veranda door. Because wildlife was so prolific there was an old pot and spanner hanging on a hook next to the door. At night, if one needed to use the loo, known as a p.k. (for pickanini kaya or little house), the provided pot and spanner were there to frighten the natural world away.
The rest of the sleeping house of course would unavoidably be awakened by the inevitable racket and the guilty party would be greeted by a general moaning and exaggerated yawns in the morning.

Mary, one night after the family were all asleep, felt an urgent need to use the p.k..
Deciding that she did not want to announce her intentions to the whole household and also not wanting to disturb the children resolved to risk a silent trip.
Clutching a candle she tip-toed out of the back door and made her way, quite successfully, to the facilities.
She entered the p.k. and eased a normally squeaky corrugated door closed as quietly as possible.

It happened just as mom got comfortable on the wooden seat.
There was a huff huff huff noise on the other side of her door accompanied by the sound of a large animal scratching itself against the rough ironwork of the little room.
Being one of Verrall's "temporary" buildings, it wasn't secured to the ground and before long one side lifted about a foot in the air. My terrified mother held her candle to the

46

new opening and peered through - just in time to see a leopard's golden eyes peering back at her before abruptly vanishing into the night.
The whole p.k. once more settled into its usual place.

Her concerns about waking the family were quickly forgotten. Only her screams exceeded in volume to the sound of an old chamber pot beating a thunderous cadence on the iron walls.

Verrall, shotgun in hand and surrounded by three very excited boys, arrived at the loo to rescue his hysterical wife.

Mom was not amused.

As her terrified account of the would be voyeur leopard progressed we yelped with laughter. Especially when Verrall, rather unsympathetically suggested that the experience was an excellent enema!
As usually happens though, karma stepped in a few nights later.

My parents had installed a large picture window in their bedroom. It stretched across one wall and was set about two feet six inches above ground and rose to just below the height of the ceiling.

It must have been about three thirty in the morning when a familiar Huff, Huff, Huff sound reverberated through the window. Wraithlike, a vague spotted image slipped in and out of view before once again vanishing into the night.

This time there was no laughing as, first thing in the morning, Verrall supervised the replacement of this window with a double strength line of brick wall.

It is also the reason we were one of the first families in our area to enjoy indoor plumbing.

Our parents' old friends, Betsy and Dries were spending a few nights with us at the farm when Verrall decided that he would take Dries to a lodge party in Ndola. As it was men only, the ladies remained at the farm with us kids. Mom and Aunty Betsy vanished into the outside kitchen after supper in order to escape the constant demands of three boys. We put ourselves to bed and I remember dozing off to the delightful smell of baking cakes intermingled with a pungent but unmistakable aroma of burning cigarettes.

I was awakened by a loud argument from the kitchen. There, under yellow paraffin light Mom was wiping blood off a dishevelled Verrall whilst Dries and Betsy looked on.
"On my word of honour" Verrall slurred.
In our family this expression was only used when one needed to be believed no matter how unlikely the story was.
"There was a lion in the road and I swerved to avoid it!"
Apparently Verrall had been driving back to the farm when he swerved to avoid a big cat. The car had rolled twice. Dries, who was asleep in the seat next to him, missed the whole thing, only waking as the car came to a stop against a large Mbango tree.
He was totally unhurt.
He had flagged down one of our neighbours who had brought the sorry pair home.

Mary, lacking any collaboration and smelling the results of a long and joyous night with friends, whiskey and beer on Verrall's breath, angrily retorted, " Don't lie to me, you were drunk and lost control admit it!"
A very hurt Verrall, now cleaned up and bandaged turned and took himself off to bed.

The next morning, his bruises now showing, my father loaded us into Mary's car and we all went to inspect the wreck.
There, the Vauxhall rested. It's until very recently elegant lines now described a horseshoe around a large tree. The ground was covered with shattered glass and various parts of Vauxhall peeped at us from behind the elephant grass. We were surprised that my father and Dries had managed to walk away from this bad wreck.
Lying on a sandy verge next to the tar road, a beer bottle, still with a remnant of liquid inside, winked accusingly in the morning sunlight..
 Mary walked up to it, "You see you could have killed Dries and yourself because of the damn beee......." She stopped in mid tirade, because, next to the beer bottle there were the pug marks of a very large lion.

And that is how Verrall got his new Triumph spitfire.

# Upside down flowers and explosions in the cinema

It was at this time that my mother, Mary, who supplied roses to florists in Ndola, became exceptionally busy. She would wake up at three in the morning to prepare the roses that had been picked on the previous afternoon for delivery. By five, the kitchen was a mass of cut stems, buckets of flowers and beautiful arrangements all overshadowed by the delightful fresh aroma of flowers mingled with burned toast.
Just about everything mom did was done extremely well – except the toast.
Our double electric toaster had no automatic off switch or pop up mechanism. It only toasted one side at a time. When that side finished then a little door had to be flipped open and the bread automatically turned for the process to be repeated. Naturally it had to be watched otherwise the bread inside would burn. This took attention, the one thing Mary did not have.

I of course did not know better and grew up believing that real toast, to be made properly, first had to be thoroughly burned and then, just before being presented for eating, scraped with a knife to reveal a slightly lighter underside.

I loved it – and still do.

When breakfast was over, mom would load her ford esquire with the day's deliveries, the kids and leave for the ten mile trek to Ndola.
After supplying her opposition, she then would go to her own florist shop and put in a full day's work. In the evening she would return to our farm, make sure everyone was fed

and then concentrate on the accounts, often getting to bed around midnight.
The weekends were different. She was able to rest enough to prepare herself for the following week's marathon.

Except for one week in July.

There were an unusually large number of celebrations in Ndola and as a result mom's flowers and services were in exceptional demand. She worked through Saturday and, whilst we slept peacefully, left at six on Sunday morning with her little car loaded to the brim with flowers.
We were awoken with my father shouting to us; "Mom's been in an accident, I'm going to see what happened!"
We all piled into the backseat of Verrall's car and sped off.
Mary was shaken, but otherwise well.
The car on the other hand, not so well. She had fallen asleep at the wheel and gone off the road not far from where Verrall had had his accident.
The esquire had rolled over several times before finally landing back on its wheels. The height of the vehicle had been altered. All the wood panelling on the outside of the car had come off and was scattered around the accident site.
Bouquets of flowers were haphazardly dotted over the entire location -just like a grave immediately after a funeral.
To me it looked like the car was a write-off.

Verrall disagreed.

With the help of a neighbour, Mary was dispatched for a check up. The loose flowers, vases and bouquets were tossed into the back of the battered car for later delivery and the esquire rescue plan began.

We tied a rope to the front bumper of Mary's car and attached it to dad's own Thames Trader panel van. The whole sorry mess was then dragged back to our farm with much groaning and rattling.

My brothers and I were made to crawl into the rear of mom's elevation challenged car, lie on our backs and place our feet on the roof. We were then instructed to push. With great effort the squashed and buckled metal eventually popped back up to its original height.
We then ripped the torn cloth upholstery off and set about taking the dents out with mallets.
The end result was a frankensteinian resemblance of mom's little green car.
"Perfect, as good as new!" my father proclaimed.
"Now for the ceiling."
A large piece of hardboard was cut to size, and once again we were instructed to push it into place with our feet, my father riveting the whole monstrosity into place.
A fresh coat of green paint was then applied.
"Its only temporary," Verrall told my horrified mother.

The amazing thing was that the esquire remained that way until Verrall sold it three years later.

So long a time, in fact, that we grew quite proprietary of our unique little car!

A Saturday visit to the local Ndola cinema every two weeks was a major highlight.
We would arrive in the redesigned esquire, our arms laden with comics in anticipation of swapping with the other similarly burdened kids.

Cole was one of the biggest boys and surrounded himself with a gang of loud and cruel friends.
Of course he couldn't resist mocking mom's readjusted car.
We were helpless to defend ourselves against the bigger boy and his gang of sycophants.

We needed a strategy.
Obviously a direct assault would be imprudent and so the exploding cigarette was devised.
At that time, to be seen with a cigarette in his mouth was the coolest thing a young boy could do.
Free smokes would be the bait.
Michael and I obtained a pack of fifty springbok from Mrs. Grey's store and got to work.
The first half inch of tobacco was carefully removed from the front of each cigarette.
In those days cap guns were the toy of choice for little boys. A paper role of tiny spots of explosive chemicals was inserted into the gun. Every time the trigger was pulled the hammer would crush a spot and there would be a satisfying bang. They were called caps.
We inserted one cap in each Springbok filer and gently replaced the tobacco.

The great day arrived.
Thankfully Michael's mum dropped us off and we managed to avoid the scorn of the other kids. We went unnoticed to Cole's favourite spot behind the box office and left the cigarettes on a chair.
As the cinema bell rang to announce that the show was beginning, one of the Cole toadies spotted our bait, looked around furtively and snatched the box up.
We all filed in as the lights dimmed.
Velvet curtains slid aside and a beam of light hit the screen.

Queen Elizabeth appeared dressed in the scarlet uniform of the royal guards. Sitting side saddle on a horse she saluted as the anthem "God save the Queen" started to play.
We all stood to attention whilst her soldiers marched past their sovereign.
After this spectacle, we all sat anticipation of the trailers and serials that were about to begin.
"BANG!" Cole exploded.
Girls squealed and ushers flashed their torches.
"BANG!"
People were getting up and rushing for the exits.
"BANG! BANG! BANG! BANG!" echoed the sycophants.
The lights went on.
Cole and his gang's saucer - like eyes appeared in sooty faces just as the last "BANG!" exploded in their midst.
The kids looked at them in astonishment.

And then began to laugh.

# Guy Fawkes

Every Guy Fawkes, we would be let loose with our friends in Kansenji. We walked around the neighbourhood with a ball of string calling at the top of our voices "Penny for the Guy, penny for the Guy" The residents of the area would then come out with their small change. In the northern Rhodesia of the fifties pennies were produced with a hole in the middle. We put this anomaly to good use, threading the string through each coin until we had a long brown worm of copper pennies attached to our line. Proof that whist some of the residents were eager to join with the spirit of Guy Fawkes, some others, I'm sure, paid up to get rid of the annoying high pitched voices from their suburb. These funds would be later utilised to finance the building of a dummy Guy Fawkes. His unhappy fate called for this mannequin to be placed on a large pile of cut wood and set alight on the 5$^{th}$ November. On Guy Fawkes Day, Verrall would also appear from Ndola carrying a large box. In it there were rockets, squibs, Catherine wheels, a few flash bombs and of course the sparklers.

The excitement would build up and finally as the sun went down we were allowed to light the bonfire whilst everyone, especially the adults, cheered, not so much because of the commemoration of the saving of the British houses of parliament, but because of the amount of alcohol consumed. About halfway through this ritual, we were allowed to start with the firecrackers.

Of course the first to be used were always the flash bombs. These small bombs were packed with gunpowder; their only purpose was to make as loud a noise as possible. If a small boy was careful, after lighting one these vicious monsters and, just before it exploded, placed an old tin over it, the tin would then be launched like a rocket to about one hundred feet in the air.

We naturally had no control where it landed.

Verrall and his guests were standing in the back garden, the celebrations in good swing when the first tin came crashing down into a tightly knit group of adults deep in boozy but earnest conversation.
Much to our enjoyment, there was a delightful panic as colonial veterans of both world wars, the Korean War and other conflicts scattered with their spouses squealing loudly.

Verrall, thoroughly exasperated banished us from the adult area and commanded us to "go and play".
His mistake of course, was to allow us to take the box full of crackers with us.

Between the house and our dairy, my father had planted bananas. They varied from the tiny lady's fingers to the huge chocolate variety. Because the banana trees were well spaced apart, it was a wonderland to run and play in.

This was also the ideal place to use the crackers. With sparklers held aloft for light we charged in and out of the plantation, throwing the squibs like hand grenades at each other.

My brother, having been the recent victim of a squib landing at his feet, and believing I was the culprit, decided on a plan of revenge – he would fire a rocket at his little sibling.

Taking three rockets from the box, he held them by their long wooden guides. In the other hand he held a flaming sparkler.
Suitably armed he began the hunt.
Soon I appeared and the chase was on. I ran in and amongst the banana trees swerving left and right in shear terror to avoid a vengeful and flaming rocket driving into me. Neil in his excitement brought his hands too close together and the sparkler set three rockets wicks alight. Stunned he stared at the looming disaster as the fuses burned down. The last picture I had was of my brother's astonished face as the still unreleased rockets whooshed and finally exploded into multi-coloured stars. Neal's silhouette appearing and vanishing in magnificent Technicolor.

My brother's screaming brought the alcohol laden adults into the banana plantation. Several of Verrall's guests landed with a wet squishing sound into the soft stems, their arms and legs impossibly intertwined with giant banana leaves. Finally some slightly bedraggled adults headed by my father finally made it to the scene of the disaster.

All the wild games and fun of Guy Fawkes ended as my unfortunate brother was carted off to Ndola hospital by now sober and very worried parents.

Whilst he carries the scars on his hands as a permanent memento of that evening so long ago, I have developed a lifelong loathing for firecrackers of any kind.

# Some culture

Verrall had decided that it was time for the family to "get some culture." We would be going to the Ndola M.O.T.H. hall for a musical show.
Even at that young age I was a lover of classical music and the opera. I imagined dramatic sword fights between duelling princes. Their weapons clashing loudly whilst encouraged by beautiful ladies with high soprano voices competing with the bearded tenors for the audience's attention. The audience sitting in their formal clothes rapt with attention. I had seen all of this at the monthly Saturday morning matinee movies we attended for one shilling entrance.
I impatiently ticked the days off until finally Saturday arrived.
Thoroughly scrubbed and dressed in our best clothes we were loaded into the car for the 10 mile trip to town.
The tall trees and elephant grass of the Northern Rhodesian bush whizzed by.
But not fast enough.
   Our excitement at the thought of our first live show kept Mary busy controlling giggling and wriggling boys in the back seat for the 20 or so minutes of the journey.
At last we pulled into the M.O.T.H. parking lot and gawked at the other arrivals.
Where were all the smart people?
Everybody was dressed casually ......except for our small family. My freshly scrubbed face, so recently given a last minute clean with Mary's freshly moistened handkerchief, turned red when, to my horror, I saw Margaret Butler, grinning at my overdressed family. She pointed to the poster stuck on the notice board which proudly proclaimed: "Saturday Only – Live. And underneath; THE BUSHCATS."

The Bushcats were known throughout the Copperbelt as a rag-tag collection of ageing men, who dressed in tramp outfits and told very bad jokes.
Nobody, except, naturally, my father would dream of getting dressed to see a performance.
　Verrall of course loved them.
Oblivious to the strange stares, he shepherded us through the foyer and to our seats near the back of the auditorium. To my relief, the lights darkened and then our ears were assailed by a horrible noise. Something like someone shaking an old paint tin full of stones. The velvet curtains parted and there was the strangest sight. A motley group of people dressed in rags were holding various odd implements. A bearded man clad in red and yellow rags stood in the middle of this group. He was holding a box with a string attached to a wooden pole. His index finger attacked the string whilst he pulled the pole back and forth, loosening and tightening the hapless cord. This weird instrument produced a monotonous THRUMMMM THRUMMM whilst the player's top hat with its broken lid like an opened jam-jar jiggled out of sync with his gyrating hips. Another band member held a washboard seriously strumming up and down the wavy metal with a small drum stick. And, yes, that was the guilty person responsible for the horrible noise. Grinning insanely and sweating profusely, he was shaking a large drum very obviously filled with stones of various sizes.
The audience clapped politely.
With a flourish, the string player let go of the vibrating string and raised his arm into the air, demanding silence as if the audience had been giving him a standing ovation.
"Allo, allo, allo!" he yelled.
And proceeded with a series of bad jokes, inaudible to us in the back.
Or so I thought……..

Verrall had a raucous but highly infectious laugh.
This usually was reserved for the most public of occasions.
"HAW, HAW, HAW!!" Verrall reverberated.
Far more interested in the source of this noise, the astonished audience turned to look.
I slid down in my seat, knowing that on Monday the entire school would know of my embarrassment.
Then the strangest thing happened. Everyone started to chuckle at my parent's weird laugh. Soon people were roaring with tears running down their faces. They were laughing with Verrall.
The Bushcats could no longer tell a bad joke.

# A musical saw

One afternoon I went with Cuckoo to visit my grandfather's grave in Ndola cemetery.
The tombstone was engraved; "Harry Albert Broughton Johnson. 1894 – 1950."
Underneath; "beloved husband and father."
We tidied his last resting place up and placed fresh flowers in the vases.
"Cuckoo, please tell me about grandpa".
My grandmother looked at the tombstone for a short while and shook her head slightly.
"He was a very good man but he went too soon."
"He used to spoil me so much. Every morning grandpa brought me a cup of tea in bed and then made my breakfast. He then went to work. In the evening when he came home he massaged my feet and prepared supper.
I wasn't allowed to do anything.

He was also a very clever man. Did you know that he was the architect who built the Duncan dry dock in Port Elizabeth?"
"The trouble with being so clever, though, was that he was always in his head which was fine – except when he drove. Often Bert would sail through stop streets without looking for other cars! If anyone came the other way they would brake and laugh, "Oh, its only old man Johnson!"
No one ever got angry with him."
Cuckoo's eyes were misty - a very unusual sight from this large Dutch lady.
She looked directly at the grave and said softly, "I miss you so much, my darling Bert."

All business, she picked the hand gardening tools up, took my hand and marched us both back to her car.

I never met my father's dad, but the stories about him were legendary, especially his saw playing abilities.

After world war two, his two sons and daughter emigrated from South Africa to the Rhodesias. Aunt Joy to Southern Rhodesia, Verrall and his elder brother, Uncle Algenon to Northern Rhodesia.
Grandfather and Cuckoo followed.
They chose to settle in Ndola, a true pioneer town in the late 1940's.

My Grandfather was an architect and so he and Verrall chose to set up as building contractors. Many of the older buildings remaining in Ndola were built by H.A.Johnson and Son.

On the weekends none of that mattered because Bert, as my grandfather was known, was sought after as a saw player.
Apparently a talented musician, his saw wailed hauntingly on many special Saturday nights. Often he would be accompanied by the maudlin singing of homesick ex pat. workers too deep in their cups.

Bert was playing at the bowling club that night.
As usual the guests arrived just in time for sundowners and began drinking in earnest. By the time he was ready to begin at seven, there were quite a few rowdy voices.
 Unintimidated he took his saw, balanced the handle between his feet and pushed the narrow end down.
Bert took a violinist's bow and drew it across the now arched saw blade. The saw keened mournfully.
The inebriated guests raised their voices determined to be heard.

Grandpa played more vigorously.
Mr.and Mrs. O'Dowd, fresh off the plane from Ireland, were sitting in the front row enjoying Bert's playing.
The Irish lady was singing along quietly, hardy audible above the drunken voices.
Her husband, seven castle lagers under his belt, was not a quiet man and his voice could be heard clearly above the unruly guests.
They looked at the newcomer and shouted to each other even more loudly. Soon even the Irishman's loud singing was drowned out.
Grandpa was smiling to himself and playing even though his saw was now inaudible.

Mr. O'Dowd was a big man with a nose that obviously had been broken in many pugilistic competitions.
His wife, well aware of her husband's very short temper and his tendency to resolve disagreements with his fists stopped singing and looked at her husband anxiously. Her eyes cast about appraising the costs of various items in the club that she knew they would be paying for once a fight erupted.
The drunkards, unaware of looming danger, were now banging tables with their hands to emphasis drunken points.
Mr.O'Dowd's chair scraped back and fell on its side.
The maddened Irishman balled his fists and stormed across the room. Mrs.O'Dowd looked appealingly at my grandpa, convinced their meagre savings were now in dire peril.
Bert, without missing a stroke of his bow, kicked a bass drum on the bandstand next to him. A deep thrum echoed through the room. Mr.O'Dowd stopped in his tracks and looked around, the inebriated conversationalists, now in a defensive position fell silent.

Grandpa lifted a finger off the saw and crooked it. A huge waiter named David put his tray down and ambled across the room. Both Irishman and drunken guests prepared for a beating as he walked towards them.
Much to their surprise he strode past and joined Bert on the stage.
He nodded at my grandfather, took a deep breath and with a tenor voice that would not have been out of place in the great opera houses of Europe began to sing. The melodic wailing saw a perfect accompliment.

You could have heard a pin drop.

Bert and David had saved yet another Saturday night and Mrs. O'Dowd preserved her savings until the next fight.

# The Herbalist's apprentice and Chiripula

My herb shop had a raised roof of small branches and grass about three feet above the ground and was supported by four rickety poles that were recovered from the *ukutema* (cutting of trees). Inside was a treasure trove of bark, leaves, roots and flowers either gathered from the forest under Shabalala's guidance or given with great solemnity from my teacher's private store at the back of his hut. Each item had a meaning and multiple uses, some special to the *abashinganga* or witchfinders but all curative because my teacher insisted my knowledge was to be focused on the healing herbs.

Banataonga's colourful cloth covered legs stretched to above the roofline of my little shop. "Cipolopolo, the *ngulu* have bewitched my child, Taonga, and she is not well." Banataonga's legs erupted with a large rasping cough and a small sweating child appeared from behind the bright cloth. With my squeaky voice attempting to be as authoritative as possible, I took *bugare*1 dried leaves and some bark from my shelves and repeated Shabalala's words; "This medicine is from far north of our land and cures the illness of sweating and heat from the ngulu who protect the small flies that live near water."-"Boil these together in water and give the mix to Taonga to drink when the sun comes up, when the sun is in the middle of the sky and when the moon first appears. Also take some tobacco and place it in a tree near the stream where you collect drinking water every day for ten days and your child will be healed."
As Banataonga and her child left throwing words of thanks over her shoulder, I saw Shabalala just within earshot pretending to be occupied in the garden, but he smiled

secretly to himself and nodded his approval to the departing mother and daughter.

Indeed, two weeks later I saw Taonga playing with her brothers in the dry dusty sand and knew the Ngulu had enjoyed her gifts.

Shabalala's pride in his apprentice was soon tarnished when one day I decided to repeat scandal I had heard about the legendary Chiripula Stephenson.

One evening, at sundowner time the adults were sitting by the tennis court chatting. I happened to be in earshot when the conversation came around to the scandalous behaviour of Chiripula Stephenson, an Englishman and the founder of Ndola. This pioneer was one of the great explorers of our region and would have been lauded except for one fault – he had gone "native".
The man had married not one, but two black women and hosted many African guests at a time when the colonials were desperate to prove their superiority above the local people.
He had delightfully named the twins in his brood of eight children Alpha and Omega and was one of the pioneers who opened up Lala land for the British colonial powers.
The scandalised colonials of the sundowner club, reluctant to give him credit for anything, dismissed this as a result of "something to do with native superstition and a pet baboon!"

My teacher was never angry for long and decided to tell me the story of Chiripula and the Lala people.
He put his *foshol (slang for spade)* down and sat on a forty four gallon drum.

"It is better that you know the truth about the Lala people."
As was his habit, he paused and pulled some tobacco from a small pouch made from the skin of a buck. The brown hairs still prominent on the untanned but well preserved piece of hide.
His eyes twinkled as he watched my impatient fidgeting, until at last he began; "There is a legend among the Lala people of the beginning of the world. Three god-brothers were dividing up the lands. One took the West and one the East before the third god-brother had a chance to take his share.
Angered, he said "I will turn into an animal and travel wherever I please and possess all land that my feet touch!" And so it was.
Now the English company from the south sent two men, Chiripula and a man known as Francis Jones to take the land for Britain."
"Chiripula had a baboon that lived with him like a brother. This baboon imitated his master and even smoked a pipe!"
Shabalala paused, filled his own pipe and lit it.
He then strutted around the vegetable patch doing his best impression of a walking baboon imitating a man and smoking a pipe. I yowled with laughter and pranced baboon-like behind him, carefully avoiding the almost ready green cabbages, carrots and peas.

We were both still laughing when he once again took his seat on the steel drum.
"The Lala people saw the two white men and the baboon from a long way off and said; "these people don't behave like strangers and smile as they go along!" Remembering their legend they told all to offer respect and food when the companions passed.

When the three arrived at the chief's hut, they promised that if the Lala people submitted to the great BSA Company, the English would offer protection from the Arab slave traders. They offered as proof the fact that they had already defeated their enemies, the Nguni. The Lala chief debated with his council of elders for a long time before he decided that as the brother- gods wanted it so, they would agree.

And so it was that the Lala people gave their land to the English!"

He looked at me sternly, "Remember Cipolopolo, amongst the people of this land we know the truth about Chiripula and his wives and the great chief he was."
I waited eagerly as; once again, he fiddled with his pipe and tobacco pouch.
"Because of his great love of Africa, he was walking to visit the land of the Nyasa when he became very ill. His friend, Tambo and a few others carried him to the nearest village, where the women took care of the white man until he was healed.
 Later he met the orphan, Loti, who was being sold for her virginity by the Yao dog, Muwandiga. Tambo asked him to marry this girl to save her from Muwandiga's schemes. Remembering the good deeds of the village women he agreed.

But it wasn't too long before he fell in love with his new wife. Soon he adopted the African way and took another wife, Mwapi.
The Lala god-chief, Chiripula, loved his African family for the rest of his life and was a man of great honour and should be respected by all!"

To emphasis this point he picked his foshol up and thumped it against the forty four gallon drum.

I now know that part of scorn that the colonials of our sundowner club was generated partly by awe and partly by fear of Chiripula Stephenson's high status amongst the locals.

## Turners farm, the bathtub and the major

It was a long walk from our smallholding to Turner's general store, but well worth the effort. Laya, the elderly, wizened and white haired counter assistant of undetermined origins would sell a newspaper cone of kapenta (small sun dried fish from the Zambezi River) and a pack of eight OK cigarettes for sixpence.

It did not matter that this horrendous tobacco mixture came from the rejects of the tobacco floors in Salisbury, Southern Rhodesia; it was enough that when one removed the unprotected cigarettes from their unfoiled cardboard box and lit the end, volumous blue smoke would billow and we were instantly transformed into the sophisticated people we saw in the cigarette adverts. World travellers, successful and free.

Michael and I made many forays onto Turners farm and had tried numerous shortcuts through the elephant grass. On one of our as yet untested routes we heard a feminine voice singing lustily.

Intrigued, we crept through the grass until we came across a small open glade. There, right in the middle of the opening, next to a tiny pond was a large galvanized bath. In it sat a glistening deep black and overweight naked lady covered in suds made from her red lifebuoy bar of soap. She was belting out a repetitive and incomprehensible tune oblivious to her two young voyeurs peeping from behind the grass. Giggling, we nudged each other delightedly entranced wondrous sight.

Soon, however, being small boys with not too big an attention span, we became bored by the monotonous singing and decided to stir things up. Aiming at the bath, Michael flicked a small stone. Unfortunately the stone went

off course and landed on the startled lady's massive left breast with a soggy thump.
 She leapt up and caught sight of the two little boys grasping their mouths trying to not laugh out loud. With an enraged shriek she gave chase with soap suds flying off her naked, wet wobbling body.
Yelling with laughter we vanished into the long grass and soon lost sight of our pursuer but not of her elephantine stomping and aggrieved, angry yelling until we reached the Mufulira road.
   As a reward, when we finally arrived at the Gray farm, we "borrowed" some springbok cigarettes from Michael's mother's reserve and, concealed behind the back of a farm rondavel, smoked, coughed and gleefully recounted our adventure endlessly.

A cloud of pipe smoke always announced Major Billingsworth, an ex Indian army soldier who could not bear the thought of settling in a small cottage in Devonshire. He instead chose the infinitely preferable British colony of Northern Rhodesia where he made his home in a large bungalow in Ndola. He regularly appeared at the farm every second Friday evening at around sun downer time. He would plonk himself into one of the deep fabric armchairs on our veranda and peer around for an available servant or child. His red sweaty face would light up if he caught a glance of either and demand, "Whiskey, but only Johnny Walker, black lable. And don't make a mistake! I can always tell. Terrified the involuntary nominated lackey scurried off and filled his order carefully, too intimidated to even think of making a mistake with the major's order. One Friday Michael and I caught the major's eye before we managed to hide.
"ANOTHER WHISKEY!" yelled the Major, pointing at five empty glasses neatly lined up before him, "and make sure

it's Johnny Walker Black Label, I drink nothing else you know!!" We scurried to the cocktail cabinet for the whiskey bottle.
"WHERE'S MY WHISKEY!!" a slurred regimental voice demanded.
Michael grabbed the neck of a bottle from the bottom shelf and hastily poured a generous dollop into a new glass; he threw some blocks of ice in and rushed off to give the major his drink. I looked at the lable which proudly proclaimed: Limosin fine brandy. I rushed around the corner to stop Michael before it was too late. Certain some dire punishment would befall us. I was just in time to hear the major reflectively staring at a half consumed glass- "I only drink Johnny Walker Black lable, you know"

    Sundowner time and tennis parties were routine in Northern Rhodesia of the fifties. Besides the Major there were always hordes of guests turning up at the farm on Friday evenings for the start of the weekend tennis and drinking parties. We were banned from joining the grown ups and were told to "go and play before supper". That of course was the problem, the more the guests celebrated the weekend, the colder and more congealed the already prepared meals became. By the time my very jolly parents remembered that kids needed to be fed, they were usually confronted with yawning, bleary eyed dirty faced offspring with very little appetite.
Reluctantly and at my father's insistence we would be seated at the table and forced to eat with the admonition, "Eat up, you know there are millions of people starving in China!" A line of reasoning that has escaped me to this day but seemed to make sense to my father.
One day, we decided that something had to be done.
The back veranda was the repository of offal from animals slaughtered for the pot. The guests' and servants food had

already been taken. All that remained was destined to be boiled up into a foul smelling concoction for the dogs. I can still see the reproachful stares the two German shepherds, Janie and Lola, gave us when confronted with this mess. Carefully we ladled generous proportions into the main crock reserved for the guests late supper. We added half a packet of Coleman's curry powder to the mix and eagerly awaited the grown ups suppertime.

I was the last child standing, my brothers long since in bed, when at last dinner was served. I studied the alcohol flushed faces as they plunged into their dinner.

Amidst the cluttering of busy knives and forks, Mrs. Bartlet, the mayor's wife, suddenly stopped chewing, her face a deeper shade of red. She took a large mouthful of wine and looked around at her fellow guests.

The silence was almost unbearable for a small tired boy. But the satisfaction of seeing the grown up's discomfort was enough to fuel my delighted anticipation.

At last her nasal voice proclaimed loudly-"Verrall, absolutely delightful, you must give me the recipe!"

Cook was bemused the next day when he was instructed to repeat the meal for us and the guests the following week!

# Cuckoo

My grandmother became Cuckoo because she would, after a few brandies, tickle us as babies under the chin and cluck, "Cuckoo, cuckoo".

Not long after the sjambok incident she moved into a flat in Ndola. Sometimes she would pick me up from Kansenji primary school in her black ford popular and take me back to her home to await my parents and a lift back to our farm.
Lunch often was a watery irish stew which she served at the kitchen counter. Cuckoo never joined me but often disappeared to "take her medicine".
One day, the thought of another irish stew a totally unattractive one, something to be put off for as long as possible, I decided to follow her into her bedroom and make conversation.
As I walked through her door, there she was with a quarter brandy bottle pressed to her lips. She hastily took the offending container from her mouth, screwed the cap on and tossed it into her wardrobe.
She glared at me whilst my grandmother debated the next course of action. I breathed a sigh of relief when she decided discretion was a better choice to violence. The picture of an old age institution looming in her mind.

Verrall had threatened to put her in a home if she continued to drink as she was "a danger to herself".
"It's just my medicine," she cooed as sweetly as possible. My grandmother had just placed a weapon into her grandson's hands!
 Cuckoo insisted on calling my school kanstenshi, much to my annoyance. No matter how I tried to correct her, she remained intractable. She would say, I will pick you up in

kanstenshi tomorrow after school. My inevitable reply always was, "No Cuckoo, Kansenji, not kanstenshi!!"
"Yes." She said, "Kanstenshi". My fingers would ball into a fist in frustration.
One day my grandmother had some chores to do before lunch and left me alone in the flat.
Bored, I went into her bedroom and lifted her bottle of "medicine" from under some clothing. Without too much thought, I took the bottle and handed it to a delighted cleaner who was standing in the passage outside her front door.

Cuckoo returned and placed a few parcels on the counter next to me. "Derek, take your lunch out of the oven, I am going for my medicine."
Increasingly desperate and noisy shuffling and searching noises emerged from the single bedroom until; "Have you seen my medicine bottle?"

"No, Cuckoo, didn't you leave it in Kanstenshi?"

On our next outing from my school my grandmother finally remembered that the area was called Kansenji.

# Five star services

At this time, amongst the several properties that Verrall owned in Ndola, there was a garage which he called Five Star Services. He had decided the motor car trade was going to be his best bet for a good business.
 Set up on a hill in Kansenji, the white painted garage had a showroom, petrol pumps and a workshop. To run the workshop, he employed a Southern Italian migrant whom we knew as Mr. Spizzo. Even though he was a first rate mechanic, he spoke no English. My father had, however, learned to speak Italian whilst serving with the South African army in Italy during world war two. Verrall would escort his customers to the workshop and then as they explained their problem, Dad would translate and soon the garage echoed with the melodic sound of Italian interspersed with English and Chilapalapa as instructions were shouted to the Bemba workers. Everyone in Ndola soon heard about the marvellous Italian mechanic and brought their broken cars to five star services. Verrall's business prospered and I was introduced, for the first time, to a different European culture.


Giordano was about my age and the eldest child of the seven Spizzo kids. Most families of that time had three, maybe four children, but never more. Verrall explained that this anomaly was because Mr. and Mrs. Spizzo were "foreign" AND Roman Catholic. Verrall also used this argument to ban me from playing with his employee's children.
 It took me many years before I fully understood his real argument. Prejudices of the colonies and the recent war ran deep.

Of course, we soon became friends and before long, I was invited to a meal at their house, a home owned by Cuckoo and built by my father and his father's construction company that had thrived until my grandfather passed away. One of the signatures of this company was the way the cement floors were floated under water for up to four weeks.

I was to find out that Mrs. Spizzo who was a large lady cooked exquisitely. Unfortunately, like her husband she spoke no English. Giordano would translate anything he felt I needed to know. My first meal at their home came as a huge shock. There were ten of us seated at the huge pine table.
None of the formalities existed. Everyone spoke at the same time, with the loudest voice claiming precedence. Hands waved, bits of food went flying off forks as vital parts of the conversation were emphasised. The delicious food was accompanied by thunderous applause and more shouting in the beautiful but incomprehensible Italian.

Suddenly a rowdy but otherwise peaceful meal abruptly increased in volume. Suddenly Mr. Spizzo leaped up and threw his chair backwards with a loud crash. It ricocheted from the wall, bounced off a small table and landed on the beautifully finished concrete floor.
Giordano, in his turn, cast his chair backwards. It described a magnificent arc before landing on its back on the same striking floor.
Giordano, accompanied by his siblings' vociferous encouragement and his mother's unintelligible yelling, charged around the table with his father in hot pursuit, shouting Italian invectives. As Giordano leapt over a recumbent chair, Mr.Spizzo, now in range, landed a resounding kick on his son's backside.

My friend yelped and continued his circuit of the table. When his father came into range, Giordano received another boot.
Suddenly, a visibly tiring Mr. Spizzo stopped, picked his chair up, sat down and recommenced his meal. Giordano with much bravado did another circuit, smirking, before also sitting down and continuing his lunch as if nothing untoward had happened.
Shell-shocked, I abruptly found my plate extremely interesting and did not look up again until another of Mrs. Spizzo's mouth-watering servings arrived.

After many delightful meals at the Spizzo residence, I soon became used to the father-son antics and joined in the fun.
Five Star Services also sold cars.
One day, my father called me, "Derek, I have to deliver the land rover to a customer in Kitwe – do you want to come with?"

Of course I did. Land Rovers were exciting vehicles that did thrilling things like drive soldiers into war.
I clambered onto the passenger seat next to Verrall and we set off on the thirty two mile trip to Kitwe.
The large rubber tyres, so differently treaded to normal cars, made a unique and strident humming as four spinning wheels attacked the tar.

A sound that even today makes me think of that journey.

"This is the same car that the police and soldiers use, isn't it, Dad?"
Verrall smiled and nodded. "But you know, in the war we used the American Jeeps".

Verrall very rarely spoke of his world war two experiences and I beamed with joy as he commenced with the story of the American helmets.
His normally very serious face relaxed and he smiled.
"We were in Cairo for a small break from the war when my friend, Theo and I managed to get our hands on some soldiers' helmets." He began.
"We spent a hard Saturday rubbing them in the sand to take the new helmet look off. We then used a fist sized rock to beat a dent in each one."
"That night, Theo and I walked into a bar that was mainly filled with American soldiers recently arrived to join in the war effort.
 My friend put his arm around me as I clutched one of the helmets and proceeded to cry. (A trick Verrall used many times later whilst delivering a particularly sad sermon!)"

Soon enough curious American soldiers were asking what was so disturbing to the South African soldier.
Theo replied that the poor man did not want to talk about it at which stage my father started to howl, clutching his recently "upgraded" helmet more tightly.
Of course, the American G.I.'s were more determined to have this sad soldier's story.
Eventually, after being plied with free beer, Theo would relent and describe the harrowing battle in which Verrall was the sole survivor. This was only because the helmet had taken a direct hit. The shock had knocked him out and thus saved his life as the fierce Germans ran through the last few standing South Africans and bayoneted all who appeared to have a breath of life in them!
The as yet untested G.I.'s, being determined for a souvenir, started bidding. Verrall hugged his helmet more tightly to his chest as if this were his last and greatest love.

Finally, as the bids began to slow down, my father relented and pocketed the money.
They repeated this as many times in as many bars until they had run out of helmets!

I often wonder how many American homes had one of those helmets in pride of place, ready to be brought out should their owners want to tell a good war story!

My father ended this tale with his trademark HAW HAW HAW!

This time just for me.

Dad regaled me with many more stories until, far too quickly, we arrived at our destination. The new owner inspected his second hand vehicle and handed over the princely sum of one hundred pounds cash in full and final payment!

I was allowed to hold this incredible amount of money as I sat in the back seat of dad's Vauxhall that Mr. Spizzo had brought to take us back to Ndola.

Sometimes, my father brought me to the service station after school and I was left to my own devices.

I soon discovered the petrol attendant's families and their children.
A small cluster of whitewashed huts had been built behind the garage as temporary accommodation for the shift working petrol attendants.

Even though there were no real facilities and workers were expected to "do their business" in the surrounding bush, it was inevitable that the labour force took up permanent residence.

Soon the little settlement was bustling with busy wives and exuberant children.
The families welcomed me and immediately I was an honorary part of the community.

As on the farm, at meal times, everyone would sit around dishes of sudsa, kapenta and the ubiquitous tomato chilli sauce. There were no implements and I was expected to use my hands, just like everyone else.
Taking a small palm full of sudsa in my right hand I would follow everyone else's lead and dip the maize meal ball into the red, dripping sauce. The sodden sphere then would be loaded with the tiny dried fish and the entire mix eaten with lip smacking relish.
I always tried to be there for this late afternoon meal, not only for the delicious food that could only be eaten with my hands, but for the joyous company of laughter and genuine caring for each other.

I knew that in spite of the terrible circumstances that most native people of the time lived under, there was always another unseen community of people that shared the space.
Shabalala had taught me how the ancestor spirits often chose to live amongst their families.
These people, although invisible to most, were just as real, their presence accepted as part of the community.

Accompanying the ancestors there were sprites and divas that played mischievous tricks. Possessions left in one place

would vanish for a while, only to appear a few hours later in a different place.
Tin cups full of water would be emptied and food sometimes disappeared.
The people laughed at these antics, just as one would indulge naughty but beloved children.

This belief system was so strong that everyone could almost disregard the discomfort of the present and enjoy the fantastic world of spirit where joy and abundance were never far away.

Life was good.

# The Dawning of UHURU

In the 1950's before any real liberation struggles began to become evident, the indigenous peoples were regarded as foolish children by their white colonial overlords. They could be superstitious, backwards and sometimes comical, but never to be totally trusted. We all took this in with our mother's milk and totally believed in our superiority without question.
In spite of my teacher's influence, it was easy to be unknowingly cruel.
  One beautiful morning, just after a rain storm, with the ground beginning to steam away the moisture, a transient dripping Bemba man appeared at our back door begging for a bite to eat in exchange for some piecework. My father, annoyed at the intrusion appeared with Janey, one of the farm German Shepherds well known to be particularly vicious and protective. With one glance at the growling dog, the man ran to one of the many trees surrounding the homestead and without apparent effort appeared to glide upwards towards the highest point. My furious father took this in and called a labourer to fetch an axe. He shouted up to the man to come down or the tree would be felled together with its terrified refugee. In desperation, the man began removing his clothes and throwing them down, crying; "Take what I own, but please do not let the dog eat me!" My brothers and I had gathered to watch the excitement and began to squeal with mirth.
Eventually, my father relented and allowed the man to descend; telling him that the now restrained Janey would be released after 10 seconds. Unclothed the poor Bemba man grabbed his meagre belongings and fled with the ominous countdown beginning….. ONE...TWO…..
On ten as promised, Janey was released and flew off in hot pursuit and vanished into the steaming undergrowth.

I do not know what happened to the poor man, but we retold this story with relish and much amusement to anyone who would listen.
The sad thing was that, at the time, everyone who listened thought the story was amusing.
One can't help reflecting on the peoples of Africa who, in their desperation to survive, have walked for thousands of kilometres, only to end up standing at robots with their hands out begging for a coin from the more affluent but generally uncaring folks at the southern end of this great continent and how time may have passed, but much still stays the same.

It was the evening before my eighth birthday and my parents were seated next to the wood encased radiogramme in the lounge. The dial had Lusaka and Salisbury printed on the glass of the medium wave section. On most nights they listened to the local radio stations broadcasting news and music, the yellow light displaying which of the two towns the signal was coming from. This night, however, the little yellow light was glowing in the shortwave section next to London.
Mom and Dad were in deep discussion and I heard the words, "Sir Harold Macmillan" and "Winds of change".

Our lives were about to change forever......

One Sunday in May, 1960 my grandmother, Cuckoo drove up to our house in her Ford Popular, the windscreen shattered and her head was bleeding. She had been on her way to the farm for lunch after bowls in Ndola and passed a burning car on the side of the road. It belonged to Mrs. Lillian Burton. She pulled up to help but a member of a large crowd gathered there raised a knobkerrie and smashed her windscreen. She lowered her head and accelerated away

from the mob. The Police were called but not in time to save Mrs. Burton, who died later in hospital, fortunately her daughters who had been with her in the car managed to hide in the bush and were unharmed but heard their mother and little dog screaming from the burning car. The car had been petrol bombed by dissatisfied native people who were calling for independence.
Eventually some of the members of the crowd were arrested. Cuckoo was called in to an identification parade where she had to touch anyone she recognised on the shoulder.
Four of these perpetrators were later hanged and Cuckoo never forgot her part in their demise. She always shuddered with distaste when she was persuaded to recount the story.

Shabalala was sombre on Monday and pulled me aside when I returned from school, "Cipolopolo, it is a very sad day for Mr Burton and his children (The Burtons were neighbours and sometimes popped over to our farm for visits) but our people are angry and wish to be free of the English. There will be much trouble, but a different future is certain. Remember you will be a healer and your anger for this family and the many things to come must not consume you. You will meet healers of Africa and you must show that it is your wish to be one of them."

# A VC10 and the good life

After the demise of the ill fated comet, we were delighted to hear that British Overseas Airways Company (B.O.A.C.) had acquired a small fleet of VC10's. They had chosen the African route to be one of the first to service with this latest and most modern of aircraft.
When the VC10's started appearing in our Northern Rhodesian sky's regularly on Sundays, the locals would pack their families into their cars and head for the viewing deck at Ndola airport.
Verrall was no exception and with great excitement we would all clamber into mom's Ford esquire and drive the twelve miles or so to Ndola airport.
Excitedly, the adults with their beers and whiskey and the children grasping coca colas and chips stood around on the concrete viewing deck. Neighbours caught up with the latest news and scandals. Kids ran around playing tag, scurrying around the adults' legs.
No one really minded though because it would soon be time for this masterpiece of modern technology to arrive.
Someone called out, I can hear something!' We all stopped our chatter and gambolling and listened carefully.
"Yes, me too!" a number of people agreed.
Finally, "There it is!" the most eagle eyed person would call out proudly, as if they had just won a major golf tournament.
We craned our necks and stared to the north. A shining dot appeared swooping towards us like a distant cattle egret that had finally spotted a likely tick laden cow.
The egret changed into a silver plane as the rumbling jet engines began to cause the deck to vibrate. Our excitement became just too much to bear and our boyish legs, as if with a will of their own began pumping up and down. Our arms, vaguely resembling a very distorted and

86

uncoordinated chongololo pointed as one to the approaching plane.

After completing a circle around the airport, almost like a victory lap after the long marathon from London, the VC10 with its four roaring engines dropped to the runway, its wheels hitting the tar in a rubbery cloud of smoke.

The plane dashed forward so fast that it seemed it would be impossible to stop in time. Four Rolls Royce engines screaming in reverse as eventually it slowed. Just in time, it seemed, as the end of Ndola airport's single runway began to run out of tar.

At a more sedate pace the blue and white liveried VC10 with B.O.A.C. emblazoned midway above oval shaped windows, taxied to its parking place allocated in pride of place in front of the arrivals door. A covered stairwell was pushed forward by three smartly turned out apron assistants. Their new uniforms issued for this momentous occasion.

With bated breath and in silence we watched as the cabin door cracked open, a white gloved hand appeared to grasp at its side. The aluminium door fully opened and a blue uniformed and very smart hostess appeared. She stood to one side as the first class passengers appeared. Smartly dressed ladies clasping their suited men's arms blinked in the early morning African light.

We did not wait to see the rest of the passengers alight as the next and greatest scramble was about to begin.

We all rushed back to our cars, competing to be the first to leave on our way back to Ndola and the awaiting chefs of our town's smartest hotel, the Rutland.

No one wanted to be excluded from a feast of freshly prepared salmon, reputedly caught the previous day in Scotland and flown out on the very same recently arrived VC10.

The adults gathered in the main lounge to await a chiming luncheon gong.
It didn't seem to matter that we kids had to wait out two hours to lunch time. We were sent to the red polished veranda where fewer formalities were required. We resumed our game of tag, this time with no adults to supervise other than the benevolent white coated and red sashed waiters. We boisterously shoved and pushed at each other until the inevitable happened. Someone, usually one of the smaller kids, unable to maintain their grip on the slippery red polished floor, catapulted with their legs spinning like an hysterical ice skater straight into some unfortunate old lady quietly attempting to enjoy her tea and scones on a Sunday morning!
The waiters, fearing the wrath of a floor manager attracted by the ruckus scooped us up and banished all the offending kids into the hotel prison- like courtyard behind the kitchens. Soon our game continued and by the time we were finally summoned for lunch, not a few of us were scratched and grazed. Our clothing in disarray and covered in a mixture of polish, blood and good African grime.
Mothers, fully aware of the consequences of leaving small boys to their own devices and heralded by the chiming dinner gong, appeared to gather their tattered offspring. They tucked shirts in, pulled socks up and wiped dirty faces with saliva wetted and Chanel perfumed handkerchiefs.
By now thoroughly hungry we suffered the undignified attentions of our mothers and then rushed to our awaiting feast in the dining room.
The hotel management, well aware of the potential disasters that could be caused by young ruffians in a five star hotel dining room, arranged for a children's table to be set slightly away from the other diners in an alcove near the kitchen.

It didn't matter, though, as we preferred to be away from our parents' reproachful eyes. The food was just as good! Finally the waiters arrived bearing the steaming first course of Scottish salmon embedded in greens, carrots and potatoes.

I would like to record how I savoured this delicacy, but it was merely fuel and a stop on the way to dessert. First, though, after the salmon we were confronted with waiters pushing small carts with the main course, Rutland hotel's speciality, in pride of place on silver platters. The imaginative chef had managed to find a continuous supply of particularly large potatoes. He hollowed them out and then placed a baby chicken together with a secret combination of bacon, herbs and spices in the centre. This was carefully baked for many hours until the whole combination fell apart when touched by a salivating guest. Verrall likened the taste, in his own inimical way, as: "The soft perfectly cooked flesh of newly made angels and carried on the feather light wings of a good French red wine." This was always accompanied by the HAW HAW HAW of his laugh when he was particularly pleased with the joke he had just told.

Unfortunately, this delight went untested by the kids table as it was considered too sophisticated for us and we were served spaghetti bolognaise instead.

We all loved the life that living on a smallholding in Northern Rhodesia brought. For the adults, long lazy weekends of tennis and sundowners with interesting friends. White coated and red sashed servants dashing to fill any need.

For us, running wild in the heavy forested and untouched lands, free to explore and maybe even come across folks who had never seen white people before. On the rare occasion that this happened, the shock on their faces was enough to brag to our town-living friends for at least a week.

But most of all the privileged life that being masters of all we surveyed brought.

One day Verrall, after a particularly dry winter when the wells were almost dry, decided to have a borehole drilled. One of his gifts was the ability to "divine" water.
He determined that this would be an appropriate time to pass this skill onto his youngest son and so I was summoned to follow my father to the orchard. Verrall took his Joseph Rogers penknife out and cut a small forked twig from one of the fruit trees and sharpened the end into a cone shaped point.
"Now, Derek, watch closely!" he commanded.
Taking the twig in both hands and with a flourish he straightened his arms in the general direction of the dairy. And so the march of the twig began.
Seemingly, as if by magic, the small branch knew in just which direction it would pull my father.
Verrall marched off, his stiffened arms stretched out in front of him. To keep up I trotted on the recently forged pathway made by my marching father.
We flattened grass paths in all directions that the mischievous twig pulled us. We stormed past the cattle sheds, the dairy and two staff villages. This, of course, piqued the interest of the village children who joined in the parade. Soon, a snake of raucous kids, led by the madly concentrating and determined Verrall marched by the kitchen window. A befuddled Mary, unable to attract my father's attention, rushed out of the house and joined us at the back of the line. Janie and Lola, always at my mother's feet exuberantly attached themselves to our

growing procession. Their delighted barking adding to the festivities.

Verrall scrunched his eyes in concentration, avoiding the hoopla behind him as the mischievous twig pulled his now flagging body back to a few yards from where we started, next to the fruit orchid.

Obligingly the twig began to bend, slowly the cone shaped tip pointed to a spot in the ground not too far from the sundowner seating area.

"AAH!" cried the astonished village children.

"BWOOF!" barked the dogs.

We had arrived at our destination, the hunt for water done.

"Forty feet deep!" My father proclaimed, scraping an X in the ground.

The show was over.

A week later Mr. Niewoudt arrived with his truck. A large crane-like drill on its back.

In no time a huge engine started and lifted the drill up with much squealing and grinding. Mr. Niewoudt pulled some leavers and a steady thud thud began as the drill drove through the ground.

Once again the noise attracted the village kids who came, this time accompanied by most of the farm staff. Soon a large crowd stood in a semicircle around the borehole machine.

The brightly clothed throng began to chatter and call to each other as Mr. Niewoudt's drill dug deeper and deeper. The merriment grew as more people arrived to see what the excitement was about.

Every ten feet our drilling expert called, "Ten feet! Twenty feet! Thirty feet!"

As the crowd looked like it was about to break into party mode, Mr. Niewoudt called, "Forty feet!" and a huge fountain of water gushed out of the ground.
Everyone clapped, large white toothy smiles shone from the multitude like a multi headed but very happy and vibrantly coloured monster.
Verrall looked around smugly as the crowd AAAH'd and the dogs BWOOF'D.

Suddenly a large shiny stone appeared through the rushing water.

The drillmaster leaned down and picked this stone up. He examined it meticulously before proclaiming; "Copper!"
Verrall rushed in and grabbed the stone, promising to add one hundred pounds to the bill if Mr. Niewoudt never spoke of copper again.
If he did, the copper mines would soon be at our farm and our home would be destroyed.

We would be masters of all we surveyed no more.

# Colonial Justice.

Verrall liked to tell the story of a popular local businessman called Wally, who, when the law finally caught up with him for tax evasion, was sentenced to spend his six month sentence in Ndola prison just across the road from the Rutland hotel.
 All his friends were outraged as he was the renowned host of a regular sundowner club of likeminded colonials. The meals were excellent and the company convivial.
Being well connected, it wasn't long before the hotel was supplying his meals and his old guests were invited to the cell for an evening of good food and company.

 Life was as it should be and all was well.

Soon Wally's cell bound sundowner club nights became notorious throughout the country and Northern Rhodesians were given to discussing the delights of the previous night's menu, always served by the innovative Rutland chef in person. There were many attempts to cajole club members for an invitation to a night in the sundowner cell.
Eventually our businessman had to be moved to a larger cell to accommodate all the new guests. Framed art and Persian carpets were brought from Wally's home and the warden lent him suitable furniture to entertain his visitors.

 It had become essential to be a cell guest to remain at the top of the social ladder.

Stefan Blignault, a South African and recent immigrant to the country, decided that in order to give his newly established electrical contracting business a boost he would approach club members for an invitation in exchange for a bribe. Becoming a cell guest definitely would introduce him to all the right people.

An original member of the sundowner club, Sir Lionel Chapman-Gower, a minor baronet remittance man and thorough reprobate, needed work done to his run down bungalow. The trouble was no contractor would touch him because he never paid for work done.
Stefan saw his chance and offered to do the work as a free service as long as Sir Lionel arranged for him to have a night in the gaol cell.
 Electrical services duly completed, Sir Lionel phoned Stefan with his thanks and to tell him that they were expecting him for supper at the Gaol. He just must please be there at 6.00pm on the dot.
Six in the evening saw Stefan at the front gate dressed in a brand new tuxedo.
A large guard arrived, "Ah, Mr. Blignault, we have been expecting you." He led Stefan into a small reception. "You understand no sharp objects such as keys, pocket knives etc. are allowed. Please place any of these in this box, they will be returned as soon as you come back out."
Stefan obliged.
The guard led him down a grey painted passage and stood aside at the door of one of the cells. He gestured to Stefan to enter. The want to be social climber stepped over the threshold and into an empty cell with some bread, fish gravy and mealie meal on a small table. "Enjoy your dinner" the guard shouted, slamming the door shut before Stefan could react.
 The next morning when Stefan was released a small band of chuckling and not entirely sober colonials cheered; "Welcome to Ndola, Old Man."

Unfortunately this story was printed in the Northern News the following day and, combined with Mr. Blignault's very vociferous protests to the governor, had the hapless Wally transferred to Lusaka prison with no more privileges for the remainder of his sentence.

Another favourite story that Verrall often told was about Jack, the local pub owner of an establishment that the Northern Rhodesian policemen stationed in Ndola often used.
He also happened to be the colonial hangman. Everybody in our small town knew this and made allowances when he had to perform his duty on some unhappy convict.
Jack would look at the old station clock above his bar counter, strip his apron off and nod at one of the regulars. Walking through the swing doors, he would quickly vanish into the sunlit street.
Anyone requiring service would then be attended to by the nominated regular, often Bushy Warrington, until Jack finally returned, his task completed.


Our little country seemed to attract black sheep, rogues and scallywags disproportionate to its size.
In order to protect the family name these usually thoroughly likeable scoundrels were sent to the colonies by their wealthy and disapproving English families.
Northern Rhodesia seemed to be at the top of the list as colony of choice for banished reprobates.
Because the families paid quite considerable bribes and stipends to keep them away from England they were called "remittance men". They would pass their days pursuing wasteful pleasures, often bored and looking for trouble.

Bushy was one of them.

One day, whilst Jack was attending to one of his convicts, a loud and brash American pushed his way through the pub's western style swing doors.

Verrall, who could not imitate accents and even so never considered this flaw a hindrance, would then launch into his version of brash Americanese, no doubt gleaned from his numerous cowboy novels; " Saay, fella, is it true that you folks have lions roamin in these here streets.
Bushy, polishing a whiskey glass behind the bar, replied in his best plummy English. "Why no, Old Boy, the wildlife wouldn't think of being seen in a town like this. We do, however have human animals darkening our streets."
"What do ya mean?" the American asked.
"Well, actually we often have a killer in this bar. Not only that, but he can frequently be seen drinking with the local police!"
"No waay!" the astonished American asked, "and do the cops know that he is a killer?"
"Of course," Bushy replied.
Repeating himself, "No Waay!"
Sighting Jack returning from his grisly task, and seizing his opportunity, "I'll bet you a fiver that the next person who walks in will be that very same killer!"
"Done!" the American growled.
Jack walked in and Bushy said with his hand outstretched, "Let me introduce you to our local hangman, Jack".

HAW, HAW HAW! Verrall roared.

## Dag Hammarskjold

One night in September, 1961, I was awoken by a distant but loud bang. I wondered what the noise was about but soon went back to sleep. In the morning, Michael and I were playing in the front garden when several excited farm labourers appeared running towards us, "Pickanini bwanas, go quickly, a plane has crashed on the charcoal burners' fields!" The charcoal burners were about six miles through dense bush from the farm, but the prospect of seeing a plane crash was too exciting an opportunity to be missed. We climbed onto our bicycles and armed with our round plastic water bottles peddled off towards the charcoal burners. Our route was a disused sandy track through heavily afforested land. The effort of pedalling through deep sand was almost too much and I stopped frequently. The sounds of little creatures echoed through the forest like small guides egging us on.
Eventually, the forest creatures fell silent and the half light enhanced the eerie and gloomy mood we felt.
Our hearts beat a little faster as the smell of burning assailed our noses.
A most astounding sight confronted us. The smoking ruins of an aeroplane lay scattered over a large area of broken trees and shrubs. A survivor, a man dressed in a suit was picking his way through the wreckage. He called to us in a strange language, but we were too shocked to reply. Just then police land rovers appeared and ominous dark suited foreigners got out. They glared threateningly. Two of the suits started towards us. I remember one individual telling the other that we were only boys and to let us alone. Terrified, we remounted our bikes and peddled as fast as we could back the way we had come..

That night the radio newscaster announced: "Early this morning, an aeroplane carrying Dag Hammarskjold, the Secretary General of the United Nations was killed in an aircraft accident whilst attempting to land at Ndola airport. There was one survivor." I was too frightened to tell my parents of my adventures and went quietly to my room. A few days later it was announced that the survivor had died in hospital.

My N'Ganga was unusually serious the next day, "Today I must make the cishimba (charm) to help the great chief who died yesterday cross over." "He is mpashi (good soul) and we must make sure he keeps us in his favour. First though I must find the cause of his death and the death of his followers on the plane. Maybe it was the ciwa (evil spirits) or maybe evil spells cast by bad people. Cipolopolo this is not the time for you to help, I must meet with the charcoal burners to purify their village and drink their beer *bwalwa bwalikilwa ne mfwa* (the beer that has been interrupted in it's fermentation by death).We must have the hunts to find the cause of death. We will then sacrifice a goat.
I will speak again after the purification ceremony." With that he turned and walked off to his hut to gather his ceremonial tools. He was not seen again for a week, much to the frustration of my father who simply believed he had decided to have a break from work.

When he returned he explained that the great chief was killed by spells cast by the ciwa spirits of white people across the sea. I was not to speak of this again as the area had been purified and the kabosha (magical rotting drug) had been caste. Therefore any more discussions were pointless.

# Congo troubles and the end of innocence

The continuing rebellion in the Congo caused great excitement but also brought the harrowing reality of war home to our young peaceful lives. Our farm bordered the Katangese province which had seceded from the rest of the Congo. This rebellion was led by Moise Tchombi and saw some of the most vicious fighting right up to the border of Northern Rhodesia.

Michael called, "Come quickly, the planes are shooting something!" We rushed to a large ant heap near the back of our farm and climbed the giant mound's sandy side to its summit about four yards above the ground.
Over the Congo border, we were entranced to see jets diving at great speeds and then firing with cannon and rockets at targets on the ground. It was too far in distance to see what they were attacking as their targets were hidden amongst the heavily treed forest. Our excitement kept us sitting there long after the planes had gone and the smoke from the fires started to diminish.
  That night my parents were busy until long after dark with guests in sombre suits, speaking with in heavily accented foreign languages. Some of the visitors were dressed in military and police uniforms. As the officials were climbing into their vehicles, my father shook hands with their leader and said; "Of course, we will help."
As their vehicles vanished down the driveway, a dusty cloud blurred the yellow electric light screwed atop the pergola.
  I had never seen my parents with such serious faces before. In spite of the shadows, I noticed a tear running down mom's cheek as Verrall spoke simply; "Boys, the war in the Congo is causing many people to run away from their

homes. That man I was speaking to was from the commission for refugees and has asked us if they could use this farm as the first gathering place for victims. I want you to help as much as possible and not to misbehave."
More than fifty years later, the pain on Dad's face still lives with me. At least as an adult and a healer I now understand that he was recalling the horrors he must have experienced whilst serving with the South African Army in world war two.

   The first car sputtered up the driveway, it was a Volkswagen beetle with blue number plates displaying a gold star. Nuns in dirty black and white habits were helped from the beetle by refugee workers. Some had to be supported by the khaki uniformed men as they were taken into our lounge. As one nun was dragged by, she did not look anything like spotlessly clean and well turned out women from the convent in Ndola where Michael went to school.
Her eyes stared wildly from a tear streaked face. The dusty robes were torn at the leg and I glimpsed a hint of bloody underclothes.
As more dust laden cars arrived the bemused aid workers were soon overwhelmed. There were people on stretchers crudely tied onto the back of vannettes, their bodies covered with dirty blood stained bandages. Bedraggled refugees were sitting wherever they could find place on the vehicles, some with crude bandages tied around their heads, others with bloody rags strapping arms and legs. Most of them though, seemed to be unhurt, just very, very tired. The refugees' incomprehensible French became louder and louder as they shouted for attention amongst the ever growing crowd. People were milling amongst the haphazardly parked cars on our front lawn waving their

hands and gesticulating desperately to the English speaking aiders.

Suddenly, Shabalala, followed by many workers from ours and the neighbouring farms appeared. As people of the Bemba nation, they had relatives on both side of the border and many of them were French speaking. I watched my teacher proudly as he took charge and soon order was regained. Black and white worked side by side and in no time ambulances had taken the wounded and all the refugees were dealt with.

This process was repeated many times over the next month and I often reflect on the fates of these poor people and how individual innocents suffer for selfish political ideals.

In fact, a few years later, I discovered that a special orphanage had been established to cope with the number of children born to the nuns raped during that awful war, just the first of many conflicts to overwhelm our small part of Africa.

## A near miss, a seduction and a sad farewell

I was in my first one on one confirmation class away from the other confirmands with the Rev. John Brooks in Ndola when I began to feel dizzy. A complaint that plagued me for many years until I was diagnosed as a sufferer of hypertension. The formidable cleric stopped with his lecture, "What's the problem?" "Father, I feel dizzy and your bookcase seems to be fading away." Alarmed, the cleric came over and examined my face closely. "Don't worry, Father, Shabalala will make it go away".
"Shabalala? Who is this person?"
Realising that the tone of the Rev. Brookes had become ominous, I covered up by explaining that our gardener, Vegetable, who was called Shabalala by the natives, was the man charged with looking after me on the farm and that he had always managed to get the right kind of help when I was not feeling well.
"Yes, I'm sure he would know where to find aspirin when needed. Come child, I will lay my hands on you and ask God for healing."

It was at this moment, I realised how close I had come to revealing Shabalala and my illicit association. My teacher would certainly have lost his job and maybe have been arrested as well......I would have to be far more careful in future to continue the secret of our association from everyone, including my parents and brothers.

Gillian was an Irish protestant girl.
I had met her when we both attended the Rev. Brook's confirmation class in Ndola.
We were selected to perform opposite each other in the year end Christmas pageant – the "ox and the Ass." I was to play the ox and the gorgeous Gillian the ass. We would

prepare together and, whenever we could, try to exclude anyone else from our rehearsals. The Saturday before the big show, we had a party for all the cast. Soon we were running around over excitedly, having filled on sugary soft drinks and boundless sweets. To impress Gillian, I performed various gymnastics. The next one being progressively more daring than its predecessor. Unfortunately, it had just rained and the mud became more slippery and churned up every time I skidded and ran until my grip on mother earth failed. I turned a glorious somersault and landed on my left outstretched hand. The pain was indescribable as, girls and showing off vanished into a pink painful cloud. Verrall was summoned and I was rushed to Ndola hospital.
X rays taken, Dr. Delaney diagnosed that I had fractured my "funny bone" and would have to have a plaster caste from my shoulder to my wrist. In order to adjust the offending arm, I was put under anaesthesia. I awoke to discover my arm in a sling and a plaster of paris caste. The worst itching I have ever experienced occurred for the entire time my arm was encased. Pens, pieces of wood and wire coat hangers were inserted under the plaster in order to scratch some relief, but this was always very temporary. Sunday the day of the big day saw me performing my part in a sling and plaster.
Gillian's solace and attention almost made it worthwhile even though my cast came off the week before the schools reopened and I did not even have the benefit of missing a few schooldays!

Her mother was the church organist and of more importance to me, drove a Heinkel "bubble car". Whenever one wished to exit or gain entry to this marvellous little car, the entire front would have to be pushed open.

My excitement was clear the first time I was invited back to their house to "play". The two of us were squeezed side by side into the single passenger seat as Mrs. Hall closed the front door. She turned the ignition and the scooter-like engine burst into life. The noise made it impossible to talk. But that was just as well. I was extremely conscious of the beautiful girl wedged up against my right side. My pre adolescent emotions causing my ears to buzz and my voice to fall silent. I was very grateful that Mrs. Hall's normal questioning manner remained unsatisfied because of the vibrating and deafening machine. I knew at that moment, that I couldn't even remember my name.

That exquisite journey ended far too soon and we were unloaded and shooed into the Hall house.

Gillian led me to the playroom and we pretended to be engrossed in an early lunch as we surreptitiously studied each other. She smiled and my world exploded. How could I have missed the pleasures of a girl's company all the years before this moment?

She asked a few questions about our studies together and pretended that she did not know the answers. Fluttering her eyes in astonishment every time I answered. I felt as though I was the wisest boy ever!

Eventually, she had a particular question that required her sitting next to me. I answered and instead of the delightful fluttering, she leaned over and kissed me almost on my mouth!

Before I could grasp what happened, she leaped up and vanished out of the room giggling. I ran after her and a delightful game of "touch" ensued. Every now and then she slowed just enough for me to feel that wonderful soft body with my fingertips before running off again. A game I could have played for much longer but was interrupted by Mrs. Hall calling that my father, with his usual bad timing, had arrived to pick me up.

This enchanting game was never to be repeated as soon after that, the Halls were called back to Ireland and my budding romance was no more.

About two month's later; I received a letter from Gillian talking about her experiences in Belfast and very soon my enjoyment of the scented letter vanished as her loathing of the Irish Catholics permeated every sentence.
This was my first experience of white on white bigotry and I realised that no matter whom we are, what creed or colour, racism is racism, and can never be justified, especially when it takes the innocence of a young girl and turns her thoughts to hatred.

 "Boys, your mother and I want to talk to you." My father beckoned us from the lounge.
"As you know, the church has always been very important to us." He looked at us carefully, "I have decided to become a priest. If you however have a problem with it, please tell me now and we will discuss it." Never in my short life had any of us dared to openly go against anything my father decided to do and we certainly were not going to start now. "Good, it's settled then, you will all move to Ndola until my studies are finished."

The move from the farm to the semi in town happened too quickly and I never did get to properly say goodbye.

The great Shaman had vanished from my young life in person, but never in spirit.

# Nyanga

At Kansenji Primary School in Ndola there was a programme for pupils to holiday in Nyanga in the then Southern Rhodesian highlands.
The black and white greyhound bus was surrounded by excited young children and tearful parents milling on the dusty grounds of the school entrance.
My only interest was how I could get to sit next to Margaret on the overnight trip. This wonder girl was the daughter of my standard three teacher and had been careful to give me shy smiles in class when nobody was looking, but just as careful to avoid me and to be fair, all the boys in public.
 Even the exiting fact that the bus had its own toilet could not contain the disappointment to an awakening boy that the trip to Nyanga was going to be with the boys separated from the girls.
The long journey transversed Northern Rhodesia North to South, the heavily forested Copperbelt area gave way to flat grasslands as we passed Kapiri Mposhi in the late afternoon with the glorious sunset burning through the red dust. To a child unused to travel, the scenery was alien and slightly unsettling as we hurtled at fifty miles per hour on the newly completed double tar road towards Lusaka and away from home. After having travelled through the night, the dawn light streamed through the bus windows and kissed the lines of fidgeting kids in front of the now not so exciting sole toilet, we crossed the border at Beit Bridge into Southern Rhodesia. The bus whizzed on, the monotony settled in, only to be slightly broken by the ever changing landscape and places with exotic sounding names: Sinoia, Salisbury, Umtali, Rusapi.
 Eventually, with the last rays of the sun, our bus began to climb into the mountains through Nyanga and past the Troutbek Inn. The alpine forest was dark and foreboding

and we arrived with relief at our final destination, the holiday camp just below world's view.

The group of children and their minders offloaded from the bus, stretching themselves and rubbing their buttocks, far too tired to be excited or to notice the chill of the fresh mountain air.

The next morning after a breakfast we began our first adventure as a group of intermingling excited pupils and teachers. I was able to stay close to a giggling Margaret on the walk up to world's view, not really noticing the remarkable scenery until suddenly, there we were. A gap in the pass opened onto a cliff edge and far below us the landscape seemed to spread forever. This small opening was called God's window and girls, teachers and friends were forgotten as I felt my first thrill of the magnitude and majesty of mountains. Even after more than half a century, each time I am confronted by mountains, the tingling that I first experienced that day returns.

At the same time a soul stirring feeling of loneliness almost overwhelmed me as I turned, expecting Shabalala to be there, as always sharing this special time with me as he had done so many times before. I cast about with my eyes, looking at the sturdy little plants that no doubt were valuable medicine and that my teacher would have demanded I repeat every detail as soon as I returned. Even though I never did get the opportunity to describe them to him, so determinedly did I burn their images into my brain, that were he to appear in my study today, I would be able to pause in my writing, look up and give a thorough description of this mountain spirit's bounty exactly as he would have expected.

Bath time in the steaming communal facilities of the chalets was always a rowdy affair with boys splashing each other and romping loudly until Mrs. Jenkins appeared, sternly silencing us all and roughly scrubbing dirty ears and faces that had been neglected until then. I am sure her matronly presence helped allay some of the inevitable homesick sniffles that were bravely averted at least until the lights went out.

  The days were full of adventures and delight with sneaked treats from the holiday resort's kitchen. The kindly cook carefully averting her eyes from the tables where she had placed the food.

On a picnic in the forest, I managed to convince Margaret to slip away on a pine cone collecting mission. Her blue eyes sparkled as we ran from tree to tree filling our sacs with large cones. Mrs. Simms would be very pleased with our haul. I was proud that my sac seemed to have the larger collection and Margaret's awe at my gathering skills. It was strange that she didn't seem to mind even though it appeared that she collected more than I did until I caught her slipping some of her cones into my bag. She looked up and laughed. Pretending to be cross I pushed her and she fell on the soft needles. She tapped my feet and I landed next to her, laughing out loud. This had to be the most amazing girl that I had ever met. Suddenly she leaned over and I experienced a fleeting brush of her lips on mine, her sweet breath lingering for just a moment before it evaporated into the forest air. My first kiss was a joy that lasted just a second before Margaret grabbed her bag and ran off to reunite with the others.

By the time I rejoined everyone the girls were gathered around Margaret and the boys were snickering. She walked up to me, smiled and took my hand – it seemed we were officially boyfriend / girlfriend!

The fun filled days melded with joy and delight but soon our holiday came to an end and before we knew it we were reversing our journey back up to Ndola.

While adventures and fun certainly were part of the holiday, the distinct smell of pine forest and clean crisp mountain air have remained with me. Especially in later life when I bought a small tree farm on a mountain in the Natal Midlands area specifically to recapture that alpine smell of the pine and freshness.

## Embarrassment and a new way of thinking

The day came for my father's ordination in a joint ceremony of confirmation and ordination. I was to read a lesson during the service and this honour terrified me no matter how I practised. The dreaded moment arrived and I stood at the lectern and gazed around fearfully. I was mortified to feel a warm trail of water running down my leg. Hoping no one could see the puddle forming at my feet I started to read.

To my surprise, I soon began to enjoy the experience and was saddened when the short reading was finished. I looked around foolishly expecting applause from the congregation but a proud smile from my mother was reward enough. I knew at that moment that one day I would give many lectures and talks.
 After the service archbishop Oliver Wilkinson and canon George Mulenga came to congratulate me; Canon Mulenga said, "Come, boy, let me introduce you to the ordinands."
 My father was not the only person to be ordained that day and to my surprise the five other new clergy were all black. To see native people in the church was very unusual, but also to have black priests in authority was a shock and was the first real evidence of the "winds of change" speech given by the British Prime minister, Sir Harold Macmillan.
 I wondered what Shabalala would have thought about it.

The first parish my father was sent to was as a locum for Rev. Peter Wilde in Luanshya on the Copperbelt. Father Wilde was on long leave in the United Kingdom and we would be there for about a year. The family was uprooted from the semi in Ndola and every few months deposited in various temporary houses in Luanshya. I was enrolled in Luanshya primary just at the time that the pop group the

Beatles were starting to make a name for themselves. In a very active youth club, my father would "twist and shout" with my classmates much to my embarrassment.

Cathy was dark haired with brown eyes and slightly more mature than her contemporaries. She was almost unapproachable by an underdeveloped new boy in class but I had managed to strike up a few conversations with her and in my imagination had her as my girlfriend.

Until the day she joined the youth club and encountered Verrall.

As usual, when the music started on the small portable gramophone, the girls would congregate on one side of the hall whilst the boys would glance surreptitiously in their direction, digging each other in the side in encouragement to be the first to cross the floor. Verrall, with his total lack of concern or aplomb, singled Cathy out from the midst of her friends and dragged her across the parquet floor and to my horror presented her to me with the command to "Show us how a young couple should dance to the Beatles!" I stood up to the quiet sniggering from both sides of the dance floor and attempted the seemingly mad and incomprehensible gyrations I had seen the older kids do. I would like to say that I naturally fell into the rhythm and wowed the crowd, especially Cathy. Just the opposite.

My much bruised ego was confronted with joyous ribbing from the boys and contempt from the girls until I left Luanshya for good about six months later.

It was impossible to escape Verrall's embarrassing ways. The school had decided that all Christian pupils needed instruction and of course, in spite of my silent prayers, the headmaster asked my parent to conduct the class.

Because most of the students were Christian, no classroom was big enough to accommodate everyone and as a result the school hall was chosen. It was built in much the same manner as school halls throughout the southern part of Africa. This half bricked building had glass French doors down either side with windows placed above at a height that required long wooden poles with brass hooks to open them. But most of all, and to my father's joy, there was a stage.

Set about three feet above the hall floor, the stage had purple velvet curtains on either side. A lectern was place precisely in the middle. Verrall, who always loved an audience, especially a captive one, gripped the sides of the lectern, looked around in what he thought a dramatic and intelligent manner. He would stare at randomly selected pupils for a few seconds and then move on to the next victim. He had decided that this was the best way to garner attention from primary school children with limited attention spans. He succeeded. But only because my fellow students were terrified into submission. Satisfied, the Reverend Verrall Johnson proceeded with the lesson. He spoke for about five minutes and suddenly, without any apparent reason, would stop and fire a question at his now beginning to bore audience. He stared expectantly at the silent children hoping for a show of hands. Instead, he was confronted with children suddenly interested in their nails, the brickwork or the ceiling. Feeling helpful, and to start the ball rolling, I raised my hand.

"Not you, Derek, I know you know the answer!"

Suddenly, everyone was looking at my red shiny face, the architecture of the school hall and dirty nails forgotten. No one sniggered though; my father was the master of embarrassment. Once a pupil was bold enough to misbehave and of course Verrall had a solution. The recalcitrant boy was called up to the stage, made to stand in a corner and shout out as loudly as possible, "Lost!"

Throughout his tenure as R.I. instructor, no one else dared to misbehave in his class.

My retreat at this time was a small windowless brick hut with a corrugated iron roof and whitewashed walls. It had previously been a store room for alcohol kept especially for various church functions. Amongst the beery smells I played my classical music collection and studied the few books placed in pride of place on a small wooden shelf. All the books were on astronomy and the sciences. I had a favourite, though; Teach yourself astronomy. The yellow and black cover was torn and its pages were dog-eared from the abuse it had suffered over the many hours that I had spent studying every word.
The big problem with this book, though, was that it had been written with readers in the Northern hemisphere in mind. Before I realised this, I had sat night after night staring at the sky trying fruitlessly to find the constellations so beautifully illustrated in my book. Perhaps the reason I never pursued my dream of becoming an astronomer! Nevertheless, this room soon became "the observatory" in my mind.
Perhaps also, for me, the reason I still associate beer with academic pursuit!

The observatory became so much more over those few months of my tenancy. I gathered herbs from gardens in the suburbs and prepared poultices and potions to my hearts content, imagining the ailments that they could cure and how a proud Shabalala stood behind me guiding my hands in their production. Occasionally, I would be brought back to reality and my eyes misted up with the knowledge that my beloved teacher was no longer there.

The rectory in Luanshya was a big house with three bedrooms and a study. It nestled amongst large trees that had matured many years previously to their full height and coverage. This was marvellous for the hot summers but had a downside. We were in effect totally isolated from our neighbours. In February, 1964 we moved in and my mother turned Father Wilde's bachelor's digs into a family home. My parents took the master bedroom on the North side and on the opposite end of the house; my brother and I shared a room.
Earl, the golden spaniel decided that the passage outside our room would be his quarters.
These arrangements suited everyone. The kids away from the parents and the parents away from the kids with an immovable dog in between.
Earl's passage led from our bedroom to our bathroom and then to the back door. A sturdy metal door with mosquito netting covering any gaps to the outside.

Every morning my brother and I would step over the sleeping dog on our way to the toilet. When Earl's breakfast was ready, one of us would be sent to wake him. Much shaking of the long golden furry dog happened before; at last, a bleary eye would open and glare balefully at us.

"Early! Come breakfast is served." Eventually, and only as a favour, the dog would go to the kitchen where his meal awaited. First, though, his long ears were tied into a knot above his head, forming a golden coronet entirely appropriate for this member of the aristocracy. There was of, course a practical reason for this. The long ears always drooped into his plate and we were tired of washing and combing his ears every time he ate.

One night, after everyone was fast asleep, the burglars came.
The house was ransacked and even our boyish possessions were not sacred. Treasures were taken and we awakened to discover gaps on tables and in our wardrobe. Verrall was on the telephone and not to long afterwards, the police arrived to find our family shattered sitting sipping tea amongst the chaos.
The policemen conducted a search from room to room, shouting to each other occasionally. "Yes, they broke in through the back door, tell the fingerprint guys to start here!" called a constable on his way to inspect our room. He appeared too soon to have reached our bedroom with a sorrowful look on his face. He looked mournfully at me, "I'm afraid the burglars have killed your dog!"
We all dashed to his passage, tears beginning to well in my eyes: "Early! Early!" I cried.

As I screeched around the passage, Earl's baleful eye was glaring at the indignity of being awoken so rudely after a peaceful and undisturbed night's sleep!

Earl wasn't a brave dog. I was playing out in the garden when I heard my mother shriek with terror. I ran into the house and there, in the lounge, I was confronted with the strangest of sights. My father was facing off with a terrified rat cornered for the moment between the wall and a Kist. He was brandishing a broom threateningly whilst looking as fierce as possible. About six feet behind him Mary stood, her hands over her mouth staring terrified at the fierce monster.
Behind her, peering through mom's legs stood Earl, his eyes like saucers!

It was apparent that his only redeeming feature was his beauty and that was enough.

## Independence

  First the countries north of us had achieved independence from their colonial masters, and then it was our turn, the Federation of Rhodesia and Nyasaland dissolved and the preparations for our own small country's journey to "Uhuru" began. There had been much fuss about the elections but not much of the violence usually associated with the normal birth pangs of an emerging African country. For me, a young boy at the start of his life, the excitement of a new country being born brought all sorts of breathless emotions. I enthusiastically learned the new national anthem based on *Nkosi Sikelel' iAfrika"* ("Lord Bless Africa" in Xhosa)*:

1. *Stand and sing of Zambia, proud and free,*
   *Land of work and joy in unity,*
   *Victors in the struggle for the right,*
   *We have won freedom's fight,*
   *All one strong and free.*

2. *Africa is our own motherland,*
   *Fashion'd with and blessed by God's good hand,*
   *Let us all her people join as one,*
   *Brothers under the sun.*
   *All one, strong and free.*

3. *One land and one nation is our cry,*
   *Dignity and peace 'neath Zambia's sky,*
   *Like our noble eagle in its flight,*
   *Zambia, praise to thee.*
   *All one, strong and free.*

*Chorus (sung after third verse only)*
*Praise be to God.Praise be, praise be, praise be,*
*Bless our great nation,Zambia,*
 *Zambia, Zambia.*
*Free men we stand*
*Under the flag of our land.*
*Zambia, praise to thee!*
*All one, strong and free.*

\* *(originally composed as a hymn in 1897 by Enoch Sontonga, a teacher at a Methodist mission school in Johannesburg, to the tune'Aberystwyth' by Joseph Parry)*

And, as instructed by that wonderful chorus, I hastily placed a pole with a paper Zambian flag atop it in front of the observatory.

On 24th October, 1964, Independence Day, we were all shuffled off to the local football stadium in Luanshya and railed by the local politicians.
I regret I cannot recall what they had to say as all I can now see in my mind's eye is the multicoloured crowd singing and ululating delightedly, all the time swaying in perfect rhythm to the beating drums.

The British flag was lowered and the Zambian Green Flag with its golden eagle above the red black and orange stripes was raised for the first time.

I have never felt so proudly and completely part of Africa as on that day.

On that day, at least, we were, indeed, all one, strong and free

# A BROKEN EAGLE

Unexpectedly at breakfast one morning, Verrall put his fork down and looked at me with a glimmer in his eyes: "I have a surprise for you, Derek. We are leaving in half an hour so hurry up and finish your food!"
Even though I knew he was expecting it, I couldn't resist, my heart beginning to beat a little faster, "What, dad? Where are we going?"
He smiled and told me to hurry up, but to remember to bring a jersey.

His parish car at the time was an old Morris minor vanette. Because of the accumulated parish paraphernalia on the seat next to him, I was forced to sit in the open back. The rattling of this little car's engine combined with the agonised squeaking and groaning of tired metal made it impossible to communicate and I was left to look at the passing streets of Luanshya, painstakingly set out by the copper mine's town planners.
Although various miners' wives had made a valiant effort with their gardens, it was impossible to ignore the sameness of the houses. It was as if some overworked architect had only had enough time to draw up one design before moving on to his next project.
Soon the houses began to thin out as we moved away from town, the overgrown vacant lots made impenetrable by the natural and ever-present Zambian bush.
I rapidly lost interest in the scenery as Verrall's little vehicle rattled and protested more loudly than ever because it had began to do battle with an unpaved road. Obviously my father was just as eager to arrive at his destination because he chose this time to increase his speed, my bottom now feeling every bump and jolt. I

grabbed the ancient sheet steel sides and grimly hung on, my concerns for my safety beginning to take precedence over my excitement of the coming surprise.
Long elephant grass on either side of the road now shortened my view to dust billowing behind the Morris. Some of it crept maliciously into my bumping, noisy world and made me sneeze.

Miraculously and at last we came to a halt safely. A very grimy and miserable little boy emerged through the dust cloud.
"Come, come!" Verrall called, vanishing around the side of a large barn like building. I followed, patting at my khaki clothing half heartedly and concentrating on clearing my eyes of the grainy dirt that threatened to scratch their surface.
"This is Mr. Blanchard and he is going to take us up today." Verrall proclaimed. I'm afraid the rest of his introduction was lost as there, behind the two adults; four Bemba men dressed in blue overalls were pushing a red painted aircraft out of the barn. The single bladed propeller stood proud in front of its lone engine.
Mr. Blanchard smiled indulgently, "Derek, you will be in the right seat today and your father will be the back seat driver!"
Verrall didn't look too happy about this but soon forgot his chagrin as we were loaded into the small plane through a door below the overhead wing. Mr Blanchard walked around the plane, touching a panel here, moving flaps up and down there, and when at last, he was satisfied, climbed in and sat behind the controls. He muttered to himself during a very brief pre flight check and finally pushed a button. Amidst a blue cloud of unburned aviation fuel, the propeller began to turn, following explosive engine backfiring.

I was relieved when the backfiring stopped and our engine roared smoothly.
"Everyone ready?" our pilot asked and without waiting for a reply pushed the throttle and our plane bumped forward over the grassy runway.

It was at this moment that I noticed that there were empty rivet holes next to me below the ancient sandblasted Perspex windows: "Where are the parachutes?" I yelled above the now roaring motor.
Mr. Blanchard smiled, gave the thumbs up and we belted down the runway. Our plane took small leaps into the air as it hit bumps in the grassy landing strip as if it was preparing itself for a final and not very trusting jump into the air. With a last thrust at the sky and just before the runway ended, we wheezed off the grass and were airborne.

Even though our stomachs remained firmly on mother earth!

As we gained altitude, the air began whistling through open rivet holes and the entire machine rattled ominously. Verrall's face had changed to a paler shade but I could see his determination to remain collected in front of his son.
"Look! There's Makoma Dam, just below on the right!" Our pilot shouted and banked the prehistoric aircraft towards that large body of water, the altitude slipping away at an alarming rate.
Verrall's teeth bared in a corpse-like grin as he nodded less than enthusiastically, his only wish to be back on terra firma.
Mr. Blanchard pulled on the rudder and we swooped up again. I'm sure that Verrall had said or done something to offend him because he took his hands off the joystick and shouted to me: "Take her and hold her steady!"

I grabbed the control and to my surprise, it held firm with no bucking or jumping. I turned to look at my now ashen father.

Just as we hit an air pocket.

The old plane dropped about one hundred feet and a shaken Mr. Blanchard grabbed the controls and headed the aircraft back for home, well aware of a very purpley faced Verrall behind him.
Nothing more was said and we were back on the runway in a few minutes!

As my father alighted, our now chastened pilot took my father's hand and shook it, "Well, Father, that was exciting, I'm sure you both had fun"

Verrall, his face, chameleon-like had changed to a blotchy green colour mumbled: "Delightful," then turned and threw up on the rubber aircraft wheel.

# Poverty begins at home

It all started with Mary and the housemaid, Margaret pulling the kitchen apart.
Mom had decided to bake some bread. It would be an excellent time to use her new mixing machine.
So, with ingredients scattered over all the kitchen work surfaces, my mother went to the pantry and took the mixer box down.
It was empty.
"Margaret!" she called. "Where is my new electric mixer?"
"Eh?" Margaret asked.
"Lo mixer" Mary said, convinced that Margaret would now have no trouble understanding.
"Eh?" Margaret asked.
Exasperated, Mary snatched a wooden spoon held it out with outstretched hands and ran around in a circle crying out; "Whirrrrr, whirrrrr! Lo mixer?"
"Eh?" said Margaret, only her innate politeness stopping her from turning her back on my demented mother and fleeing.
I walked in as my mother began to clear cupboards, scattering kitchen implements everywhere.
Margaret, in desperation, and in an effort to please her mistress who was so obviously expressing her insane side, also began emptying cupboards with vigour.
"What are you doing?" I asked.
Mom stood up from her mad cabinet emptying spree and looked at me with slightly wild eyes,
"Lo mi...." she began, getting ready to perform her mixer imitation again.

She stopped, realising she wasn't addressing Margaret, "I mean, Derek, I can't find my new mixer! We've looked everywhere with no luck."

"Oh. Didn't dad tell you? He took it to the car muttering something about the poor Randalls. He also filled a bag of food from the pantry before he left."

There was a silence and Mary's face began to get thunderous. I fled, feeling a sudden fear for my father's wellbeing.

I was playing in the front garden when Verrall arrived home. Still in his cassock he sprung up the stairs calling, "Mary! How about some tea?"

This was too good an opportunity to miss. I snuck up behind him and stood out of sight behind the front door.

My father collapsed into his favourite chair, blowing air out his mouth dramatically, "You would never believe what I've just done!"

A teacup crashed down, the liquid spilling over the lip and onto the little stinkwood "riempie" side table.

I looked around the door frame just in time to see Margaret beating a hasty retreat towards the back door whilst Mary stood over Verrall brandishing her wooden spoon. The wild look had returned to her eyes, just with a little bit of fury added for good measure.

Verrall, now in terrified defence mode said with a voice now almost an octave higher; "I didn't do...." He stopped because he had no idea what he didn't do.

"You stole my mixer!" Mary fumed.

A light of understanding crossed my father's eyes. "Oh that!" he said.

"Poor Mrs. Randall came to me for help. Her drunkard husband has left her and the kids. Before going he sold everything for drink!" He looked at my mom indignantly, "So I borrowed a few things from the house just to tide them over until they can get on their feet".
It was safe to get a closer look, so I walked in to the lounge.
He eyed me speculatively, "Pity you're not a girl, the Randall kids could do with new clothes. Perhaps I'll ask the Reeds to donate some of their daughter's dresses…."
He stopped and looked at his wife's still smouldering eyes. "Don't worry, Mary I'll organise another mixer!"

And so he did.
A relatively unscathed electric mixer appeared after a considerate parishioner passed away and left a few household utensils to my father.
Mom didn't have to worry about the mixer's age though because it too, in its time, found a new home with another needy parishioner.

Verrall had set a new standard and my mother would never again be sure what she actually had in her home.

Just that it was always enough.

# A holiday

The end of the year arrived and with it many new changes to my life.
Verrall was given his first parish in Mufulira and I was enrolled in my first high school. I was to be a boarder at St.Stephen's College, in Balla Balla, Rhodesia.
   But first, Verrall packed Mary, me and my brother, Neil, into the small Ford esquire station wagon for a two month's stint of leave to Port Elizabeth in the Eastern Cape, South Africa. The journey from Luanshya, across Zambia, Rhodesia and South Africa would take five days. Our little car tended to overheat regularly so there were regular stops in which we could stretch our legs and, at least for a short while, have a break from the claustrophobic confines of the car. Mom always would have hard boiled eggs and hot tea available for these stops. It was with great gusto that we ate the eggs, knowing that they would have a satisfactory gaseous effect on our stomachs. Sooner or later the car sounded to the tympanic blasts of escaping gas from all of us, much to the hooting delight of the two boys on the backseat.
In Wankie game reserve in Rhodesia, we stopped to look at a pride of lions that were sunbathing. Because our pride was so close to the road, Verrall thought it prudent to keep the engine running in case we became too tasty looking for the lions to resist.
Unfortunately, it wasn't long before the esquire had had enough. The engine died amid great clouds of steam. Once again our little car had overheated.
We decided to remain in the car until it cooled down. Perhaps the lions would move away after a while and we could get out stretching our legs. At least to give Verrall time to adjust whatever he needed to in order to get the car to start again. After an interminable hour's wait, the

temperature gauge showed that it was finally o.k. to start the car.
Verrall tuned the ignition key and pulled the starter button......nothing.
When this happened there was only one thing to do. With a spanner kept for just such an occasion, Verrall would get out, open the bonnet and virtually climb into the engine compartment, leaning over the wheel house at an angle that pointed his bottom in a direction facing the sky. The appropriate engine part would then receive a resounding thump from the spanner and, if we were lucky, it would come to life. There was only way into this part of the engine and it was from the driver's side - the same side that faced the non moving pride of lions.
By this time we were all demanding to "go to the toilet" and crying that we couldn't wait anymore.
There was only one thing to do. Verrall, seizing his spanner, leaped out of the car slamming the door with alacrity. He opened the bonnet and dived into the engine compartment. As expected his bottom pointed straight at the lions and I'm sure I saw it twitch in fear!
Nevertheless, the repair was done in record time and a very flushed Verrall plopped back into his seat.
Mary finally had had enough and threatened, at the next garage; to load the boys and herself onto the next train and meet Verrall in Port Elizabeth should he not fix the car.

Verrall, being famous for his temporary repairs using unlikely materials "until I can get it done permanently" did not let us down. At the next small town, he disappeared into a general dealer's and emerged about a half an hour later with an asbestos pot stand peeping out of a paper bag. With the air of a true professional, he opened the bonnet of the esquire and set to work, pieces of wire and asbestos soon were persuaded to take on the unnatural forms of weird engine parts. At last he invited us to inspect his handywork and sure enough he had devised an air scoop around the recalcitrant water pump and, to his credit, we never had an overheating problem for the rest of our holiday.

In fact and to the best of my knowledge that little car spent the rest of it's working life with the temporary asbestos pot stand relieving the water pump of it's excessive heat.

In 1964, roads were generally strip or single lanes stretching for long distances between the sparse towns. There were a few farms along the way but often there was nothing separating the road from the untamed African bush.

Somewhere in the southern part of Rhodesia while we were having our tea and boiled eggs, a small herd of giraffe loped past us totally unaffected by the presence of five wide eyed humans. We did not realise how fortunate we were to experience the last of the truly free roaming animals of Africa just before their home territories finally succumbed to the plough and the domestic cow.

It was on the third morning of our journey that, at last, we arrived at the Rhodesia/South Africa border. Having passed through customs we said farewell to Rhodesia and crossed a steel bridge over the mighty Limpopo River. The width of the water was impressive, but we had seen big rivers before, not the least being our own Zambezi. What was special, though, was the sight of a hippopotamus swimming down the middle of the river, scattering a small group of crocodiles in his wake.

Truly the King of the river.

Our trip south took us through the northern Transvaal. The great wide open spaces of the farms allowed a view not so often seen anymore. The sun rising that morning still stays with me so many years later and I can appreciate why a part of South Africa not too far from here was renamed Mpumalanga, the Zulu word for the place where the sun comes from.

Mary's little Ford esquire raced the sun for a final stretch of that day's journey. We were scheduled to spend the night with my mother's nephew and the oldest of all of our cousins, John, in Irene Pretoria.
Verrall, deciding that he needed to replace his energy lost on the marathon from a now very distant Beit Bridge, stopped for a short break.
While Mary once again offered the ubiquitous boiled eggs and tea, Verrall, out of sight of his wife, slipped a tepid beer from the cooler box and guzzled it down as quickly as possible.
Even in those hard drinking days of the colonies, it was well known that alcohol and driving were not a good combination.
"VERRALL!" Mary shouted.
This indeed was a new phenomenon; my normally docile mother never raised her voice.
"Put that beer down now!" she commanded. Verrall took a quick last sip and threw the bottle in our trash bag, relieved that he had managed to finish the golden liquid before being caught.
In a an heroic attempt to stay out of trouble, he explained that, he had heard that the alcohol, taken in just the amount that he had just consumed, helped revive tired motorists- and it had certainly worked in his case.

A frosty silence pervaded the car for the rest of our trip to John's house.

My parents were talking to each other the next morning. We made an early start- "because of the rush hour".

Dad had a choice; go the long way around Johannesburg or straight through the middle, technically a much shorter route.
Verrall, of course, decided to go the "short" way.
"Don't worry, Mary, I was here during the war and I know the way well!" No one dared to tell him that world war two had been over for nearly twenty years and of course the city must have changed, as cities tend to do.
After travelling the open country between Pretoria and Johannesburg the first signs of the city started to appear. Houses, at first scattered, soon began to get closer and closer together as the yards became smaller and smaller. Shops and flats made their appearance. Unfortunately so did the number of cars.
Verrall began to look nervous as intersection after intersection whizzed by.
Mary, knowing how Verrall's "short cuts" normally turned out, had a map spread out on her lap, trying to find where we were. Stubborn as ever, he refused to ask directions until twenty minutes later, he admitted, "I think I missed my turn. Mary can you point me back in the right direction, I will then take us straight out of town".
Mom snorted and peered at the road names. Most were long and sometimes in incomprehensible Afrikaans.
"Ah, here we are." Mary sighed and pointed to a large sign. "City of Randburg" it proclaimed. Verrall nodded knowingly, "of course". My mother glared at him, "You don't have a clue, do you!" "Just a little lost", Verrall admitted slowing down and searching hopefully for a sign that some well wishing Randburg official had placed for just such an occasion and proclaiming- The Johnsons, just right here for six hundred and fifty kilometres, to get to Port Elizabeth.. !"

Unfortunately his search was in vain.

Rush hour cars had now began to build up and their angry hooters shouted loud protests, not making any allowances for our foreign registered Esquire.
I wailed "I want to weeee!" pointing significantly at my lower regions- "NOW!"
Fortunately for the traffic behind us and the about to be moistened back seat, a Caltex garage appeared and Verrall turned off.

I don't know what was said, but when I reappeared from the service station toilets, a chastened Verrall was seated in the passenger's seat and Mary firmly ensconced behind the steering wheel.
She obviously knew were to go and after another half hour or so, countryside appeared and at last, we were back on the road to Port Elizabeth.

Verrall took the wheel again.

In spite of our trepidation, no more beer was consumed and no wrong turns were made and a day later, the little car with our exhausted family arrived at "the hill".

There was, about fifty kilometres north on the road to Port Elizabeth, a rise in the land that one had to transverse before one could begin the descent to the city itself. When we approached this small hill, the excitement level grew as at the top we first glimpsed the sea. Verrall slowed the car and we competed to be the first to shout; "The Sea, the Sea!"
There would be no stopping now, because after 5 days on the road, all we could think of was the waiting tidal pool at the Willows holiday resort.

The Willows resort was about 15 kilometres outside the city itself along a windy road that was an extension of Marine drive. On both sides of the road the city had planted Port Jackson willows in order to stabilise the dunes. The willow trees exuded a particular odour that was not unfamiliar to us from the North – similar to the smell of a dying Matabele ant when squashed. As soon as we had booked into our thatched rondavel, we grabbed our swimming costumes and plunged into the tidal pool. The feel of the buoyant seawater on our bodies brought home the fact that yes; we had survived the trip and were truly at the sea!

Margaret was the blue eyed, blond daughter of the caretaker of the resort. She was my age and we soon formed a relationship. Her smile was enough to make me feel that I was the luckiest boy on earth. Our favourite place was lying in the sun on the sandy beach and we would spend hours wrapped up in each other to the exclusion of all others – until my eldest brother, Neil joined us one day. He was six years my senior with a magnificent "Duck-tail" haircut. Within no time Margaret was hanging on every word the older boy uttered. My thoughts turned to dark revenge. It didn't matter that Neil was not interested in my love because she was far too young, all that mattered that I had lost her wonderful attention to an unassailable rival.

One morning, Neil was sunbathing on the beach and fell asleep in the sun, his near naked body continued to cook as I sneaked away from the sun's bright glare.

Later, in the afternoon, a bright red brother appeared at the rondavel, barely able to walk. The next day his skin began to very painfully bubble and peel and he was banned from going outdoors.

With Margaret back, I must admit that I felt very little remorse for not waking my sibling timeously.

Even with a delightful young girl's attentions, I often wished that Shabalala, the man who knew so much, would have been able to join me at the beach. I wondered what he would have thought of the endless sea. I had tried to explain it to him and how the ships that sailed on it were much bigger than several houses. His polite attentions to my words were always accompanied by total disbelief and dismissal as the ramblings of a small boy's fertile imagination.

I though about how I could show him some of the wonders I encountered and captured a small shellfish and carefully placed it in a soda bottle filled with seawater. The bottle was tightly corked and I gave it to my father with the instructions to find Shabalala when he drove past our old farm on his way to Mufulira.

Just as well Verrall never managed to find my mentor as by the time he passed the farm all that remained of the poor creature was a shell bobbing miserably in its briny water solution.

134

# The Family

My mother's eldest sister, Aunt Elize Wilkins, her husband, Uncle Bob and their two sons Keith and Atholl lived on a smallholding about ten kilometres outside Port Elizabeth. They were Jehovah's witnesses and as a result, Verrall was very concerned that we may become "corrupted" and so any visit to the Wilkins was carefully supervised. No matter where we roamed on the smallholding, Verrall could be seen furtively watching from a vantage point not too far away in case we took to the road to convert neighbours. Of course, this was a challenge and we in our turn kept an eye on my father for an opportunity to rebel.

In order to save precious water, Aunt Elize had a sea water tap installed by the municipality. She would use this water for many different purposes but never for human consumption.
Verrall, one day, while observing from a vantage point in the kitchen, unthinkingly took a glass and filled it up from the seawater tap. Without looking he brought is up to his mouth and took a long draught.
An almighty ruckus broke out as fresh water was given to him by a giggling Mother and her sister. This infuriated my parent even more and it was quite some time before he could resume his vigil.

We were nowhere to be seen.

Summoning the other adults it wasn't long before he had formed a posse. They searched the house and grounds of the small farm, even looking under the long tables in Aunt Elize's violet greenhouse.
To no avail.

He dashed to Mom's Ford esquire, loaded Uncle Bob and began to patrol the neighbourhood. Soon enough he came across our receding figures as we walked up the driveway of a neighbour's farm. Under our arms we carried pamphlet sized paper.
The family car, roaring in hot pursuit, screeched to a halt next to us. An apoplectic father leaped out the little car, and, leaving the door ajar stormed up to us, certain that the devil would be not too far away. He seized the paper, grabbing a sheet and held it up: "What do you think you are doing with this rubbish?" he yelled.
Innocently we pointed at the blank paper that we had gathered from Uncle Bob's office; "We were just delivering this blank paper for Uncle Bob who had promised it to his neighbour's kids to draw on".
A red faced Bob agreed that he had, indeed, promised the paper.

I sometimes wonder what Verrall would have done if he had found out about Shabalala's tutorage.


Later in life, when all white boys were required to do national military service, Keith, because of his faith, became a conscientious objector. Every now and then the military police would show up at his house with an arrest warrant. They threw him in the back of their police van and off he went to detention barracks. He would serve whatever sentence he had received and return home. He never complained about the harsh treatment meted out by the contemptuous military prison warders and indeed, the ridicule from his fellow citizens. I shamefully admit that I was one of them. I don't know how many years he stoically endured the wrath of the apartheid state, but I do know

that he never buckled, steadfast in his resolve to under no circumstances choose the easier route.
I had lost contact with my cousin before I finally realised what a true hero Keith was and regret that I have never had the chance to apologise to him in person.

Harry, my mother's father who insisted on being called Oupa, lived in a small cottage in the suburb of Walmer, Port Elizabeth.
In his later life, he would have no interest in "modern rubbish" and refused to use anything but candlelight in his home. "That new electricity ruins your eyes!" he used to say.
Perhaps he was right, because he had perfect eyesight his entire life.
Oupa called Verrall "die englesman" a huge insult in my grandfather's eyes. He was heard muttering to Aunt Elize that the only decent thing my father had ever done was to give him grandchildren!
Whenever Oupa had to be driven anywhere, Verrall tried to find a way to escape because should the car exceed thirty kilometres per hour, my grandfather would yell; "Stadig (Afrikaans for Slow down), you are travelling faster that a racehorse!"
Although a Frenchman, he had chosen to side with the Boers in the second Boer war. Thirty two years old, Oupa joined the so called Cape Rebels and rode off to battle. If he had been caught by the British he surly would have been hanged.
He loved to tell the story of how, whenever there were large family gatherings, the brothers, some on the British side and some on the side of the Boers would mount up on their horses and meet at the family homestead in Humansdorp, in the Eastern Cape. They were well known partiers and their celebrations were legendary; the

inebriated brothers were sometimes seen wandering arm in arm down the town street singing lustily.

At the end of the get-together, bleary eyed siblings mounted their horses and rode off to once again rejoin their respective and opposing forces!
I often imagined Oupa and my Great Uncles shooting at the very brothers they were arm in arm with the previous day!

Harry used to regale us grandkids with amazing stories of ox wagon parties at the Storms River mouth and how he and his friends once, after a particularly celebratory bash, managed to haul an old wagon to the top of Feather market hall in Port Elizabeth just for fun.
The old man retired with the help of a large inheritance at forty five. By the time he was sixty he had spent his fortune and was forced to go back to work. He was a door to door salesman until he retired thirty six years later at the age of ninety six!

It was during his first ever visit to a hospital that he finally expired at the age of one hundred and six.

# Off to school

At the end of January, just before my 13th birthday I was at last on my way to boarding school. I went for a swim and then hugged Margaret, stealing a last kiss. I promised that I would write every week. In my heart, though, I knew I probably would move on and our time together, as sweet as it was, could never be repeated.
 My heavy metal trunk, filled with newly bought clothing from the huge department stores in Main Street was painted black with the words boldly in white carefully, but rather amateurishly, stencilled on by Verrall; DEREK JOHNSON, ST.STEPHEN'S COLLEGE, BALLA BALLA, RHODESIA. The Willows were a fast fading memory as the car pulled onto the main road towards the station. I took a last breath of the Port Jackson Willow aroma and then we really were on our way.
 The reality of the train waiting at Port Elizabeth station to take me to Rhodesia caused butterflies to start madly attacking the lining of my stomach with their tiny wings. The red and faded yellow carriages glistened with droplets from the early morning shower. As I solemnly shook Verrall's hand and hugged my mother tearfully, I knew that for the first time in my life, I was no longer to be considered a small child with no responsibilities. I would in future have to largely make decisions on my own; I had become responsible for myself and my actions. My parents faded into a small stick insect with two legs waving in the air, the train picked up speed, white smoke billowed out it's funnel as the high pitched whistle bade farewell to the last scattered houses on the outskirts of Port Elizabeth. We were on our way to De Aar where my part of the

train was to be coupled to the Cape Town express for its journey to Johannesburg.

Soon we were in the Karoo.
The stunted thorn trees becoming fewer and fewer as the day advanced. I remembered the stories I had heard about the traditional Karoo healers, the *bossiedokters* and their wonderful dry land remedies. Of the "kankerbossie" (*sutherlandia fruitescens*) first found in the Sutherland region of the Great Karoo and used as a cancer cure. The exotic devil's claw to be used as an anti-inflammatory. I knew that one day I would have to return to study these amazing medicines.
 Lunch was announced by the tuneful chimes of the mini xylophone that a steward with starched white jacket over black trousers beat with his small rubber hammer as he marched through the train merrily calling out in English and Afrikaans; "Eerste sitting-first sitting!".
It was at lunch that I first experienced the delights of a meal in the dining car of a long distance train. The crisp white linen and porcelain plates with blue stencilled designs proudly proclaiming SAR&H on their rims offset the beautiful dark stained wooden panels that lined the carriage. The stewards fussed importantly flourishing first a bowl of cream of tomato soup and then the main course of roasted meats and vegetables. Pudding was followed by tea presented in old pewter teapots. After lunch I returned to my compartment to rest in the heat of the afternoon.
No sooner had I woken up from my lazy mid afternoon snooze than the steward was back calling passengers to tea.
The excitement of my first long train trip would not have been as enjoyable for a twelve year old boy

travelling alone had it not been for my carriage steward, Colin. He made it his personal mission to keep me company whenever he could. He regaled me with stories of his adventures as a working member of a travelling hotel.

Originally an English speaking boy from Durban and very keen to join the hotel industry, he travelled to Switzerland to train as a hotel manager. On his return he tried to get a job with a hotel in Johannesburg. It was just at this time that South Africa, newly independent from Britain, was beginning to experience ostracisation from the rest of the world because of its racial policies. In order to placate its electorate, the government ordered that a job quota in favour of Afrikaners the, until recently, mainly farming community be compulsory. My friend found it impossible to get a job in his chosen career. Strangely enough, though, because of the high number of Afrikaners working as railway stewards, the quota worked in his favour and he was able to gain employment.

We travelled to De Aar where we lost our engine and linked up to the train from Cape Town. Then on to Kimberly where the train stopped for a few hours.

It was lunch time and I thought that I would try a meal at the local station restaurant.

It wasn't much to look at. Through the door in a corner, out of date magazines hanging limply as if they no longer had the strength to hold themselves up stood in a wire card stand. A sign screwed on the third shelf proclaimed that the whole contraption had been sponsored by Volksblad, a newspaper based in Bloemfontein.

The tables were covered with cheap plastic tablecloths, printed with faded red and blue checks. In the middle

of the cloth stood a cluster of condiments. Next to little salt and pepper containers made of glass and topped with perforated stainless steel caps stood a grimy red glass bottle containing All Gold tomato sauce and a yellow squeezable mustard container of indeterminate manufacturing origin. I was about to flee when a large, very intimidating but very bored lady perched on a stool behind a sweet counter looked up and called out; "kan ek Hulp? – can I help?" She frowned at me obviously not impressed by prepubescent boys of any species. But especially, English speakers.
"P.p.pie gravy and chips, please." I stuttered, after reading the first thing on the menu written in chalk on a board above her head.
She gestured to one of the soiled tables threateningly, "Sit!"

I sat.

It didn't take long for the dreaded meal to arrive but I used my time wisely, planning the quick disposal of the no doubt disgusting meal and escaping before the large lady had time to come out from behind her counter and collar me.
There was an empty box not too far behind me, next to the magazine stand. If I waited until she was preoccupied with cleaning her nails or perhaps doing some make-up, I might just make it.
The "Tannie" appeared from behind her counter with a white plate. She slammed it down in front of me and stood back, leaning against her little counter. I feared for the counter, but even more, with a sinking heart, I feared for my health. I would have to eat the toxic waste in front of me because she just stared malevolently, not taking her eyes off me for a second

"EAT!" she commanded. I looked down at a mess of chips and pie covered liberally in thick black gravy. In order to try and oblige and in the hope that she would be satisfied with my obvious attempt to eat, I poured a little tomato sauce into the middle of the gravy.
The dragon Tannie did not buy this and merely stared directly at me. There were no more escapes-nothing left to do but eat.
Gingerly I cut into the pie speared a morsel and attached some chips to the already loaded fork.
I closed my eyes as a precaution against copious watering and placed the food into my mouth.
The strangest thing happened. A delicious taste permeated my mouth, causing my stomach to rumble to hasten the food's passage down my throat. I beamed with pleasure and wolfed the rest of my meal down, occasionally making little mmmmm sounds.
The Tannie smiled knowingly; "Everyone has the same reaction to Sarie's pies"
Satisfied, she turned and walked back to her station behind the counter.
I must admit that since that day, I have always tried to order pie, gravy and chips if ever I see it on a restaurant menu.
Unfortunately, nobody has come close to Sarie in the last fifty years.
A few hours later we were off again, this time on the way to Johannesburg.

Johannesburg station was a bewildering melee of people. Obviously Johannesburgers were very busy because everyone was in a hurry, bustling their way forward through the crowds. I didn't dare to move from my carriage.

Colin, off duty now, stayed with me whilst my carriage was once again shunted onto another train headed for Bulawayo, Rhodesia.
My last memory of this kindly steward was of his receding white coated figure standing on a platform in Johannesburg station.

He never moved until my train finally vanished into the distance.

We crossed the Botswana border and passed the capitol, Gaberones during the night.
Francistown, in northern Botswana was our first stop. The train was surrounded by hundreds of raggedly dressed children who scrabbled good naturedly in the dust when a passenger threw a penny towards their outstretched hands.
Soon many of my fellow travellers wanted to get in on the act and a rain of pennies, fruit and sweets descended on the now squealing children. Their little bodies covered in dust as they competed for the treasure.
When we pulled away they stopped jostling and ran after the departing train, big wide toothy smiles as they waved goodbye to us all.

Amidst so much poverty the amount of joy the people of Africa express is a constant source of mystery to me.

Soon we crossed another border this time for the final occasion.
We were in Rhodesia and Bulawayo, The great Matabele king, Lobengula's nineteenth century capitol, was just a few hours away.

Nearly at my final destination, I changed trains once more for the Balla Balla express – a misnomer of giant magnitude as this ancient locomotive stopped at every siding and wheezed up the many hills at walking pace. The forty mile journey took eight hours in the hot unairconditioned carriages to reach the Balla Balla hamlet.

Our arrival was not greeted with any fuss. A prefect nodded cursorily and growled that we would have to walk the one and a half miles to our new college. The bus had broken down and would only return the next day to pick our trunks up.

Thus, humping my kit bag and dressed in grey flannel trousers, white shirt, tie and blazer I walked the dusty path, climbed over a barbed wire fence and finally arrived at St. Stephen's College.

I had finally completed the last leg of my first unaccompanied journey across three countries.

# St.Stephens

The stone and cement buildings of the college were forbidding and cold under their corrugated iron roof. Prefects took charge and led us to our allocated houses. I was to be in Tracey which was across a large quadrangle surrounded on three sides by grey buildings. Our house was adjoined to a multi arched passageway that ran the entire length of one of the sides. The whole appearance conspired to look as forbidding and unwelcoming as possible. Soon we were standing in the washroom surrounded by white basins, toilet doors and the entrance to the shower room.

As Wiley the prefect for our section was talking, it became too much for my 12 year old constitution and I could feel the uncomfortable rising of my last meal into my throat. I rushed towards the toilet with my hand firmly clasped over my mouth, Unfortunately I was destined to not complete my journey and the contents of my stomach voided violently through my mouth. To my mortification, the floor was covered in my detritus and the delighted other boys immediately allocated the nickname Puke to me.

A name that stayed with me well into the first term until my sporting prowess earned a new nickname.
In the mid 1960's the Rhodesian Education department used The British G.C.E. system where a student could stay at school through the various levels from "O" to "A" and then on to "S" or scholarship level. This in effect meant that St.Stephen's College catered for boys from about twelve to twenty one years old. An impossible age difference to cope with in any social system. Especially a boys' boarding school.

Thus the seniority system was devised and tacitly agreed to by the staff. Any boy was not allowed to speak to a pupil from a more advanced class.
Being the lowest of the low in form one we were allocated to the prefects as "skivvies", our job being to clean up, polish shoes and making beds or anything the "senior" skivvies from the class above told us to do.
One day Jon and I were making our prefect's bed when I noticed some blood on the sheets.
"See Rob cut himself".
Jon studied the blood carefully and pronounced with great authority, "No, he is having his period!"
Although we were all in a mutual state of ignorance about the opposite sex, no boy would openly admit to this.
Coming from a home where there were three sons and the word "sex" was regarded as a swearword, I was particularly nescient.

I nodded sagely in agreement.

Homesickness attacked all of the new boys and even some of the older pupils. Any conversation about home was fraught with danger. If one made a remark that was even mildly derogatory, the consequences could be dire.
On 1st April, 1965, I was sitting in a geography class being taught by a teacher commonly called "Rat" by all the students. We thought it would be a good idea to catch the hated teacher with an April fools joke. A plastic bucket was filled with water, we carefully placed it above the classroom door and awaited our teacher's arrival in anticipation.

"Johnson," a familiar voice called from the window, "please take that bucket off the door so that we may get on with your lessons!"

Rat was too experienced a teacher to be fooled. Later in the lesson, our teacher suddenly looked up from his book and said to Thixton, a fellow pupil, "Look, Thixton, isn't that your parent's car pulling up?" A very homesick little boy leaped up and ran to the back classroom window. He searched the grounds frantically but to no avail. Finally he turned and looked questioningly at the master.

"April fool!" Rat cried.
Once again this master had earned his nickname. It would take a while but we were determined to seek revenge.

The next day, once again seated in the hated master's class, Rat looked away from the blackboard and glanced out of the window, "Johnson," aren't those your parents?" Hell, it wasn't even April Fools' Day and the idiot was attempting to catch me!
I ignored him, determined to not get caught by the wily teacher.
Our teacher glared at me, "Johnson, are you deaf, boy. I said your parents are here to see you!"
Reluctantly, but too intimidated to take Rat on, I twisted in my seat and looked out the window.

The little green ford esquire was parked on the sandy lot behind our classroom.

I leaped up and ran out of the door. Mom's arms were open as I flew into them, tears running down my face. I

turned and saw Verrall. For the first time in my memory I ran and hugged him. He tried unsuccessfully to conceal his joy as he gave me a small, almost embarrassed hug in return. I know now that as a child, he had been taught by his Victorian parents that "cowboys don't cry and men do not show affection!' Our visit took place in the grounds as there were no facilities for parental visits and, besides, I was not really permitted to miss class.
No matter, it was a short visit anyway. My parents had only stopped at the college on their route back from Port Elizabeth to Mufulira, Zambia.

Rat was a housemaster who lived very close to the dormitories. This seemed a perfect opportunity for young boys with revenge on our minds to seek retribution.

So we started to plot.

Everything we discussed seemed either too far fetched or improbable to succeed... until one of his most recent victims, Thixton, came up with a suggestion that was entirely fitting. We would catch a rat and under the cover of darkness, thrust it through Rat's main bedroom window. But not before it had time to become really smelly. We would tie a ribbon around its neck so there could be no mistaking that it was a gift from his caring students.
The fateful night finally arrived. It was after midnight when we gathered the plastic bag up and sneaked into Rat's garden. We knew our route very well and managed to reach the window with no problems. Jon threw it over the sill and through the window. It landed with a strange crinkling sound.

We held our breaths but there was no reaction and we snuck back to our dormitory.
All was well.

Until Rat's French class in the morning.

The classroom smelled of dead rat and there in pride of place on Jon's desk was the previous night's rat. A neatly tied ribbon on its neck and lying on a crinkly piece of paper.
I don't know how he knew Jon was involved but once again we learned that this teacher was far more canny than estimated and we would have to be far sneakier in the future. And so began a four year campaign against this master.

In the meantime poor Jon had a caning and ten hours of detention to look forward to.

The teaching staff at St.Stephen's were very well qualified and generally from good English universities. Unfortunately some of them were eccentric as well.

Our headmaster, Mr.Campbell, an ex rugby star and highly qualified for the job was also the teacher responsible for my ancient Greek studies.
Lessons took place at eight in the morning, straight after chapel.
Because I was the only student, the venue was inside his private home, in his study.
My teacher would open the front door in his pyjamas and yawning lead the way to his study. I would be sat down in an armchair close to his and the lesson would begin. The huge man stared at me balefully, questioning my interpretation of some vague and

obscure sentence written in the original Greek alphabet. If I did not get it precisely correctly, he would lean over and with his morning breath unwashed away, demand I repeat the offending sentence, this time accurately.

Even though, to this day, I associate ancient Greek with bad breath and bleary eyes, my love for the great classics has never diminished.


Every year St.Stephen's had three academic terms of about three months each. Our day started early with prep from six in the morning until breakfast.
Chapel followed and then we were in class until lunch. After lunch there was a compulsory rest period and then back to class. From four in the afternoon we had sports and then a quick shower before supper. After supper we returned to prep until bed at nine thirty.
We did not have public holidays and our weekends were filled with academic studies and sport.
The only real break we experienced was once a month on a Sunday when we were permitted to travel to Bulawayo to visit friends and relatives.
Nothing was ever allowed to get in the way of this precious time, not even food poisoning. One Saturday before the precious "Exeat" Sunday, the kitchens served tainted food that had many of the pupils dashing to the "thirty two seater", a long building that housed communal toilets. For the first time in my experience of this horrendous building, pupils were jumping up and down outside occupied stalls clasping their neither regions and crossing their legs. All the while desperate voices from the highest treble to the deepest bass

plead with the occupants of the various stalls to hurry up.
On Sunday morning the cramping tummies had not abated for many of us and, knowing that we would not be allowed out on the bus to Bulawayo, we grimaced and pretended that we were cured as we passed Rat's pre boarding inspection.

I, however, had a plan.
About an hour before the dreaded inspection, I snuck into the maths class and lifted a stick of white chalk which I consumed.
The taste of that chalk still lives with me whenever I use a chalk board in my lectures.
My plan worked and soon I no longer felt the urgent pressing of nature calling.
In fact the calling vanished well into the week!
The other boys however were not so foresighted and before the bus even left the grounds, pupils were yelling at the bus driver to stop, rushing behind the nearest bush to complete their business.
Soon however, we realised that at the rate the bus was making forward progress to Bulawayo, we would have to turn around and return to school almost immediately. The only solution would be to squat on the lowest step and hang out of the door whilst desperately clasping the two stainless steel handrails of the speeding bus.
And so it was that for the rest of the forty miles to Bulawayo boys were to be seen with their naked buttock exposed through the door doing their business often to the astonishment of passing motorists and pedestrians alike.

But we never missed our day of freedom.

# Balla Balla service station

Our weekly allowance was five shillings. This applied to all the boys and thus there was a permanent and mutual shortage of funds.
Being a confirmed smoker and 20 Peter Stuyvesant cigarettes costing a shilling for a pack, I decided that the best thing to do was to club resources with Jon and Shawn, also confirmed smokers.
The only shop that would sell cigarettes to boys was the local Balla Balla Service station which was normally out of bounds. Our solution was to get up when everyone else was asleep and cross the darkened fields for the mile long walk to Balla Balla services station. The best time we discovered was about two in the morning.
 The appointed hour arrived and I found myself being shaken awake by a groggy Shawn.
"Come on" he whispered, "It's time to go."
 The three partners in crime, Shawn, Jon and I had mutually chosen to wear school tracksuits. They were mainly black and thus more difficult to spot at night. It made no difference to us that the shoulder section had a large yellow band!
 I slipped into my camouflage outfit which I had placed under my pillow in preparation for our escapade.
We crept out of the darkened dormitory, through the washrooms and out across the quadrangle. Stealthily, our three crouched figures tip toed past the chaplain's cottage that adjoined the head boy's flat, our takkied feet leaving tracks on the sandy school road and through the barbed wire fence, careful to not snag any clothing.
 There are few places in Africa where one could not find a winding footpath and the bush outside the school was no different. We were very grateful because the

local Acacia trees had long thorns. When accidentally walked into, they could be very painful. The *khakibos* that grew at knee height also tended to shed its small and innumerable thorny seeds onto any item of clothing that brushed up against it. Evidence to the laundry staff that a transgressing boy had been wondering in the bush!
Eventually the brightly lit petrol station appeared and, after transversing yet another barbed wire fence, we were there.
We called in loud, furtive whispers, our breath forming misty blotches on the glass panels of French door leading to the shop/cashier's booth. Finally, the attendant, who slept behind the counter, staggered into view and peered through the metal double door.
 He was a tall man dressed in a crumpled boiler suit with a beaded white black and red necklace and shod in black hobnailed boots. His knitted balaclava hat was slightly skewed, partly concealing the left side of his face. This gave him a wild mad man look as he glared through the woollen threads covering his eye.
"He!" he exploded.
Shawn, the boldest of us, said nervously, "We come for cigarettes and coke…..er….we have money". This part was said triumphantly and we thought enough to justify waking the man.
The visibly annoyed Matabele man raised his hand, the bead and animal skin bracelet on his wrist in view for just a second before he vanished without a word into the depths of the darkened shop. We looked at each other with wide eyes, not sure whether to run or stay. The decision was taken from us as he reappeared with the ordered cigarettes and two one litre bottles of coke.

"Five shillings!" he growled. Although this was far too expensive, none of us were willing to argue. I produced the money and held it up. The door was unlocked and opened just wide enough to allow him to snatch the coins and pass our booty to us. The door slammed shut and once again the wild man vanished.
The other two already had their cigarettes alight. "Cummon, the smokes are getting stale!" Jon called. Shawn sniggered as I stared into the dark shop.
My glassy reflection bounced back at me and I resolved to return alone the following night.

# Gambo

Gambo was his name. I discovered this after; once again, at two in the morning I made the bushy journey to Balla Balla service station.
When his annoyed and sleepy face appeared at the glass door panel I immediately apologised for waking him saying, "Baba, I am sorry for waking you once more. I do not speak your language, but my teacher, the Bemba N'Ganga, Shabalala, instructed me to seek a Sangoma wherever I found myself for I need to learn the multiple ways of Africa. Last night I saw your wrist band and necklace and I see you as a Sangoma.
"Heh!" Gambo said. He shook his head and asked me, "Who is Mwali?"
"The great god who is protected by the Sangomas of the Matopos," I replied.
"Where did you do *uTwasa*?"
"In Zambia, near Ndola and where a patient spoke of his cure in English, a language he had never learned."
(This was one of the prerequisites for qualification as a Sangoma)
"But you are just a white boy who lacks respect by disturbing his elders in the night, why do you seek this knowledge?"
I replied, dropping Shabalala's name into the conversation as many times as I dared, that this was the task the Zambian Sangomas had given me. For, I had been told, not too far in the future, all the peoples of Southern Africa would need healers of all races if there was to be any chance of peace for the peoples of Southern Africa.

Gambo straightened his balaclava helmet and eyed me as if I were some strange unknowable creature. "I will throw the bones and consult my ancestors. Come back in two weeks." With that he closed the door, turned on his heels and vanished into the darkness of the service station shop. I didn't have the chance to tell Gambo that I would but first, I had to go Zambia for our four week school holidays. A lapse that I would later regret.

## A new town and School holidays

The train trip to Ndola from Balla Balla took two days. The forty year old engine and carriages reminiscent of a more elegant era pulled out of Bulawayo station on their way, once again, on the long journey north, traversing some of the great plains of North West Rhodesia and running next to the Wanki game reserve.   Mighty elephants inscrutably watched this great noisy smelly beast as it passed just on the other side of the game fence, leaving blue coal smoke to offend their delicate membranes long after it had vanished into the late afternoon sun. Then across Victoria Falls Bridge and into Zambia, my home country. The African customs officials, recently appointed to replace the departing colonials were proud in their new uniforms and delighted to welcome us home. Joyous laughter greeted my Zambian passport, recently issued in Lusaka and sent to me by registered mail. The number 310 printed in bold black ink below the gold embossed and as yet unfaded Zambian coat of arms.
We passed Lusaka, the capitol, as we slept, finally exhausted, our excited minds vanquished by the soothing clackity clack of the wheels monotonously turning on the iron rails.
We were awakened early in the morning. The steward's left hand held a xylophone as he beat random notes with a little rubber mallet delicately poised in his right hand. "First sitting, first sitting!" he called out, his purposeful stride covering the short distance of the sleeping car corridor as he marched down the train, exhorting passengers to the delights of breakfast, to be eaten in the mahogany lined dining car. As excited as I was, it was still impossible to resist, the toast, jam, bacon and eggs presented on sparkling crockery, still labelled "Rhodesia

Railways" in spite of our train belonging to the newly independent Zambia. Crisp napery folded into impressive cones added to a marvellous sense of occasion. We were not just eating breakfast; we were celebrating the great pioneer traditions as the African morning blurred past.
Ndola appeared in the distance, I could wait no longer; I hadn't seen my parents for the three months of a St.Stephen's term. Verrall and Mary would be at the station to greet me. We would then drive the thirty four miles to Mufulira, a place that I had not visited but would still be my home town.
The arrival was as exciting as anticipated as my parents appeared through the steam and smoke of the decelerating train. All five foot one inches of Mary was standing on her tip toes peering through each carriage window as the coaches rattled slowly past them. I just enjoyed the moment, watching my beloved parents looking for me just a little apprehensively, their half smiles ready to leap into full grins when they saw me. I must admit a small tear emerged in the corner of my eye as I tried to maintain casual disinterest in front of the other boys.
With a great hissing and squealing of metal on metal the train sighed to a halt. The driver gave one last toot on the whistle as if to say, "Well done old girl, we made it; time for a little rest before we do it all over again.
 "Mom! Dad!" all decorum was lost as I leapt from the carriage and ran to my mother. I embraced her tearily before solemnly shaking Verrall's hand.
We were soon out of the station and loaded into my father's new simca station wagon. The registration EH103 proudly proclaiming the fact that we were now from Mufulira.
For the first ten miles of the journey from Ndola I chattered excitedly. Telling, with just a little prudent censorship, of my adventures over the past three months.

Suddenly, on the left, the Tudor Inn appeared, its out of place half timbered Shakespearian façade, uncomfortably sitting in the middle of the heavily forested and still untouched Zambian countryside. We were just two miles away from our old farm, the memories rushed through my mind, one adventure replacing another before I had time to fully experience them.
There it was, a black painted sign hanging from an ornately decorated pole, proudly proclaiming the name "Broughton". Our middle name shared with the farm's nomenclature.
We were silent as we passed, no one choosing to make a remark as it would be too painful to return to those joyous times.

Our maudlin silence soon vanished when, after a further twenty miles, Mufulira appeared. Earlie (Officially and rather pompously named The Earl of Rosalind by the thoroughbred breeders) the golden spaniel was in the driveway of my new home and he washed the last sadness away. His long ears gently slapping my cheeks as his wet tongue licked whatever skin he could find.
Before I could unpack, Verrall told me that on the following Saturday I would be playing cricket for the "Away" Mufulira side. In his usual manner my irrepressible father had bragged about my cricketing prowess. He forgot to mention that I had only made the St.Stephen's under thirteen team. Not a great achievement since there were only 114 boys in the entire school and barely enough to fill the quota of eleven required to field a team.
Saturday was only two days way, and since there was no time to practise with my new team, I would be virginal as my new whites were donned.
 Saturday arrived too soon and our captain lost the toss. We were ordered to field and I was placed in the "Silly mid on"

position. The bowler was soon in his rhythm, evilly eying the other team's opening batsman as he plunged down the pitch, releasing his ball at an alarming rate. The batsman swung as hard as he could. Even as an amateur I realised that the ball had connected to the bat's "sweet spot". It took off from the bat directly in my direction. I quickly realised the reason why my position was called "silly". There was no way I could escape the brutally hit cricket ball as it sped dangerously at my head. I held my hands out in front of me to protect my face. The ball rocketed into my palms and instinctively I closed my hands around the little red beast. The resounding "HOWZAT!" echoed from my team-mates more than compensated for the wildly stinging sensation in my palms.

No matter that, when my team went in to bat and I only scored one run, I was still regarded as the hero of the day. I am however; grateful that I did not have the opportunity to play again as my later experiences in cricket proved that this would not be my medium to greatness.

   Another of Verrall's enthusiastic promotions of his youngest son's abilities also got me into trouble. Having been in choirs most of my life and even having sung on Northern Rhodesian radio once inflated Verrall's opinion of my talents. When he was asked who to recommend to sing at a wedding he was officiating, he leaped at the chance of nominating me.

The problem was that my voice had started to break and tended to vary in pitch from tenor to soprano at the most importunate of times.

I begged, even forcing my voices timbre to change whilst I pleaded for a rain check. I suggested Vicky, a contemporary of mine who had sung beautifully many times in St.Mary's. Verrall considered this and I thought I was off the hook.......Until he announced that he had arranged with Vicky to join me on the podium for a duet.

The dreaded day arrived and once again I stood in front of a packed congregation. The loving couple must have been rapped in themselves, confident that the duet would make their wedding exceptional. I don't know because I was terrified, Vicky holding my hand for comfort in vain as I shook and sweated.
The organist played the introductory bars and the entire congregation looked at us expectantly. Vicky's magnificent voice filled the church and it was as if the angels had decided to join us. I opened my mouth and thankfully began to sing passably. About one third of the way through, unfortunately my part began to sound like the braying of a donkey. There was an uncomfortable silence broken by the occasional cough from various congregants. Then Vicky's angelic voice once again reverberated around the auditorium. Sensibly I stopped singing and let the angel next to me finish.
The mother of the bride however, was very generous when she presented us both with an engraved parker pen as a reward for our efforts. She was however, later heard to remark that my singing was just like my father's. I also appeared to have the ability to stop any song in its tracks just by opening my mouth.

Whilst his passion and enthusiasm was unquestionable, Verrall, as with his raucous laugh, stopped congregants in mid voice to listen astounded to his off
key interpretation of whatever hymn was playing. To keep his hands occupied he would swing his girdle in a circle, punctuating each off key syllable with one revolution. Once, a hymn required the worshipers to "praise him" three times, each "praise him" being slightly higher than the last. "Praaiiise him!" Verrall bellowed, his girdle spinning joyously.

Even louder; "PRAAAAISE HIMMM!' Oblivious to the fact that he was now singing solo.
The girdle, at this point describing circles of impressive diameter; "PRAAAA...."

The music stopped.

Mr.Fellows, a voluntary organist and professional musician, gathered his music and stormed out of the church.

Verrall's girdle hung limply as a bewildered father, for once without voice, looked on helplessly.

# The clergymen.

Oliver Green-Wilkinson was a very thin man.
He was also the Anglican Archbishop of Rhodesia and Nyasaland.
Verrall loved to tell the story of how, when Oliver visited the parish of Kitwe on the Copperbelt he and canon "Tubby" Eaton returned late one night from their ecumenical responsibilities which had involved copious amounts of red wine.
Father Tubby was aptly named for his huge girth and jolly manner. He was large in his ways and everything associated with him tended to be oversize.
 He had a German shepherd, Sheena, a particularly large representative of her species, who lived in the vicarage with the bachelor priest.
   After midnight on the night mentioned the archbishop and the cannon arrived home very weary with only thoughts of a good night's sleep.
   Fumbling in his cassock pockets the obese cleric confessed, "My lord, I am afraid to say that I do not have the keys to the rectory. I must have left them inside the house when we left and the latch automatically locked the door."
 After giving their predicament some consideration, Tubby decided," Father, the toilet window is open and we can climb through there and open the house." The archbishop smiled his relief but it was short-lived because Tubby continued-"Obviously I am too large to gain entry." Indicating his large girth to emphasise his point.  "I am sorry, my lord but because you are better proportioned, you will have to climb through the window". Bishop Oliver graciously agreed and with Tubby providing a lift up with his hands joined under Oliver's feet the archbishop easily slipped through the open window...until he was halfway. At

that point Sheena, sensing the commotion came to investigate. Angrily she growled and snarled threateningly at the intruder arriving unceremoniously through the toilet window. Oliver, alarmed by the fierce dog yelled and tried to force his way back through the way he came. Tubby, hearing, my lord's protesting and feeling the resistance decided that the bishop was stuck and proceeded to push harder. This soon turned into a battle with the terrified bishop sawing back and forward until at last the commotion raised the neighbour who came rushing to the two priests' rescue.
Verrall's loud raucous laugh "HAW HAW HAW" would reverberate as he delivered his punch line;
"Tubby sheepishly took the proffered spare key from his neighbour. Having to confess to the bishop now back on terra firma that he had provided the neighbour with a spare key as this was not the first time he had locked himself out!"


Tubby had his revenge though.
Because of his duties, the unfortunate Archbishop was a great traveller and it was Verrall's turn to host Oliver. After a social in St. Mary's church hall, it was again very late and time to lock up. Verrall, assuming Mary had driven the Bishop back to the vicarage, locked all the doors and switched off the lights.
He, then, in his turn, sat in his car and drove the two miles through Mufulira to his rectory.

"Where is Oliver?" Mary asked Verrall who was busy hanging up his cassock.
 "Didn't you bring him home?" Verrall, decidedly worried asked.

"No he went to the church to say a prayer before coming home. I thought you knew that and would give him a lift!"

The plaintive wail, "Help, help, get me out of here!" emerged from the church as Verrall's car screeched to a halt in front of St. Mary's.

Oliver had an unfortunate habit. No matter what he was fed, he would always find some morsel to surreptitiously remove from his mouth with his fork. This he would delicately place on the side of his plate where it remained accusingly until the end of the meal. His various hostesses had tried unsuccessfully to devise meals that had nothing that the bishop would find as unappetising as to caste something aside for all to see. They would cook the best quality foods for the maximum time, but to no avail. They had tried plying him with huge glasses of wine to mellow his fastidious pallet but again to no avail.

Mary devised a plan. She would only provide soup the night Oliver ate at the rectory. We all eyed the archbishop as he confronted Mary's soup. With a slurp Oliver savoured his meal and smiled approvingly at my relieved mother….until very, carefully, he removed the remains of one of the lizards that lived upside down on the ceiling of the vicarage kitchen and carefully placed it on the side of his plate!

Oliver wasn't renowned for his good driving. One day he was crossing the recently completed Kariba dam wall from Southern Rhodesia into Northern Rhodesia. His passengers were all priests catching lifts to their various parishes on the Copperbelt. The splendour of the dam was riveting and the clergymen were suitably silent in as they sat awestruck for their whole trip across Kariba wall. On the Northern

Rhodesian side, the archbishop started to chuckle to himself.

"My lord, why are you laughing?" ventured one of the priests rather pompously. "Was it the magnificence of this wonderful engineering? I know that the splendour of the dam certainly affected us all deeply."

Oliver shook his head and said, "No, I was praying."

But, Father, that was entirely appropriate, but why were you laughing?" he asked again.

My Lord the archbishop replied: "Because I closed my eyes for the entire crossing!"

A few years later he was killed in a car accident and I'm sure, would have thought it an entirely appropriate way to go.

# A return journey

All too soon the school holidays were over. Verrall bundled Mary and I into the simca and we reversed our journey to Ndola railway station.

The energy around the about to depart train was heavy in the air. The old Rhodesia Railways badge had vanished and in its place, a newly stencilled Zambia Railways logo proudly proclaimed that at last Zambia had taken its independence in all ways. No longer a part of the Federation of Rhodesia and Nyasaland, but a new nation on its own two feet.

 The smell of freshly laundered sheets wafted from carriage compartments to mix with cigarette smoke, fresh paint and the sweaty odour of flustered porters.
We were loaded on board with teary farewells and before we knew it our loved ones had faded into the steam and smoke of the departing train, its whistle somehow sounded melancholic as it tooted a final farewell to Ndola.

As our train passed the goods yards on the outskirts of Ndola, we were confronted with the strangest of sights; two railway employees were squatted next to the slowly moving train. They each held a little hammer with which they struck the passing wheels. T. Ting rang the hammer blows. T.ting over and over. Suddenly there was a T. Tonnnng. The worker quickly extracted a piece of chalk and marked the offending wheel.
Later on the steward explained that the train had metal "tyres" and if one was coming loose the change in pitch warned the tappers. They marked the wheel for repair on their next trip to the workshops.

Inevitably we named these workers Tapiologists, a name that has stayed with me to this day.

Our last stop in Zambia was Livingston and I was soon the victim of an old tradition. I was required by the seniors to stand next to a wheel and pretend I was attaching an air pump to the steel "tyre". Then I had to make appropriate "whooshing" sounds accompanied by my pretending to pump up and down.
Anyone who questioned my strange action had to be told that the train could not leave until all the tyres were at the right pressure.
I was busy performing my strange task much to the merriment of my fellow but more senior pupils when I was approached by a man wearing a pin striped suit, carrying a leather briefcase and a pair of plain glass lensed spectacles on his nose.
He was wearing no shoes.
Before he could ask me what I was doing I blurted; "Why aren't you wearing any shoes?"
With the simplest of African logic, he replied, "My shoes are in the briefcase, I have come a long way and did not want to ruin the leather and my polish job. It took me many hours of hard work to get these shoes so shiny.
The train wheel pumping was no longer as embarrassing as I was confronted with a man who treasured his shoes so much that a little embarrassment was meaningless in order to protect something so valuable.

I thought of my trunk in the back of our train stuffed full of clothes that I had never even considered as anything of value and was ashamed.

All too soon, we were back in motion, pulling away from Livingstone station and onto the Victoria Falls Bridge.

The Zambezi River was in full flood. I heard a steward shout above the river's mighty roar that the water was plunging at more than twelve hundred cubic meters a second. We leaned out of the train window, attempting to see the Devil's Cauldron, more than one hundred and eight meters below.
A misty spray rebounded from the torrent so furiously that we could not see the swirling, raging waters as they gathered themselves for the long journey on to Mozambique and the Indian Ocean.
Unaware of being drenched, we stared in awe at this incredible spectacle.

Incongruously, about thirty meters from the top a small tree stood all alone, clinging to a rock. The flow rushed by on either side as if Mother Nature parted the furious water as a reward to a little tree's tenacity and determination to survive.

Truly, the Tokaleya Tonga words "Mosi-oa-tunya" or "The smoke that thunders." were entirely appropriate.

The Rhodesian customs officials dressed in whites like naval officers boarded our train at Victoria Falls station.
Passports were once again stamped and we were officially back in Rhodesia.
 Feeling a weird sense of loss and aloneness I stared out my window as the now distant Zambian bush faded into a shimmering haze of the hot afternoon sun.

 Soon, we would be back at school and the holiday a distant memory as the St.Stephen's routine enveloped us all.

# A Shamanic dismissal

There was one thing to look forward to, though;

Gambo.

It was a hot evening as I once again sneaked out of the dormitory, across the quad and over the fence.
The cicadas were calling and the bush surrounding the path was alive with nocturnal life. An entirely appropriate night for a meeting with a new shaman. I listened carefully and heard an owl calling. I was convinced that this was a good omen and imagined the teachings I would receive from the Ndebele Sangoma. Carefully, I climbed the barbed wire fence behind the Balla Balla service station and stepped into the spotlight over the little shop door.
"Gambo!" I called as loudly as I dared. Again, "Gambo!" when there was no response. I tapped on the glass door, "Gambo!" I called again.

"He said you were a rude boy," a strange voice said from the innards of the garage shop. A strange man dressed in his official petrol company uniform emerged. He told me that Gambo had waited for me every night after the two weeks had elapsed but I had not appeared as arranged. The month end had come, Gambo, his notice period served had returned to his village near the Matopos.
I never knew what his decision had been, just that and opportunity was lost and to this day my knowledge of the Ndebele shamanic ways is merely that which could be gleaned from the few books I found on the subject.
I have developed a lifetime loathing of tardiness.

## U.D.I.

On the 11th November, 1965, we were summoned to the dining hall to hear an important radio announcement. The room was silent. Solemnly, all the staff filed in and took their places at the extra tables that had been set in front of the stage.
We sat at our normal benches. For once there was none of our usual jostling and whispering. My stomach butterflies were in full flight as I looked around and saw that radios had been set up at strategic positions around us.
The headmaster told us to listen carefully as this was something that we would remember for the rest of our lives. He then nodded to the prefects who turned the radios on.
 After an introduction by a commentator, Mr. Ian Smith's voice echoed tinnily and crackled through the speakers. He told his fellow Rhodesians that all attempts to reach a settlement with the British government had failed.
 I remember him saying that "There can be no solution to our racial problems while African Nationalists believe that, provided they stirred up sufficient trouble, they will be able to blackmail the British Government into bringing about a miracle on their behalf by handing the country over to irresponsible rule."
Therefore he was announcing a Unilateral Declaration of Independence.

Portentously he ended with the words, "God bless you all"

And so, as Shabalala had predicted, the inexorable and inevitable change continued to unfold as the next phase of turmoil to confront our small part of Africa began.

Unfortunately the road to change would be scattered with the pointless slaughter of so many young lives. Even some members of the congregation of boys assembled that day would be sacrificed before the unavoidable transformation took place.

We would never be the same again.